LEADERS SUCCEED TOGETHER

Angela C. Crawford, Ph.D.

Leaders SUCCEED together

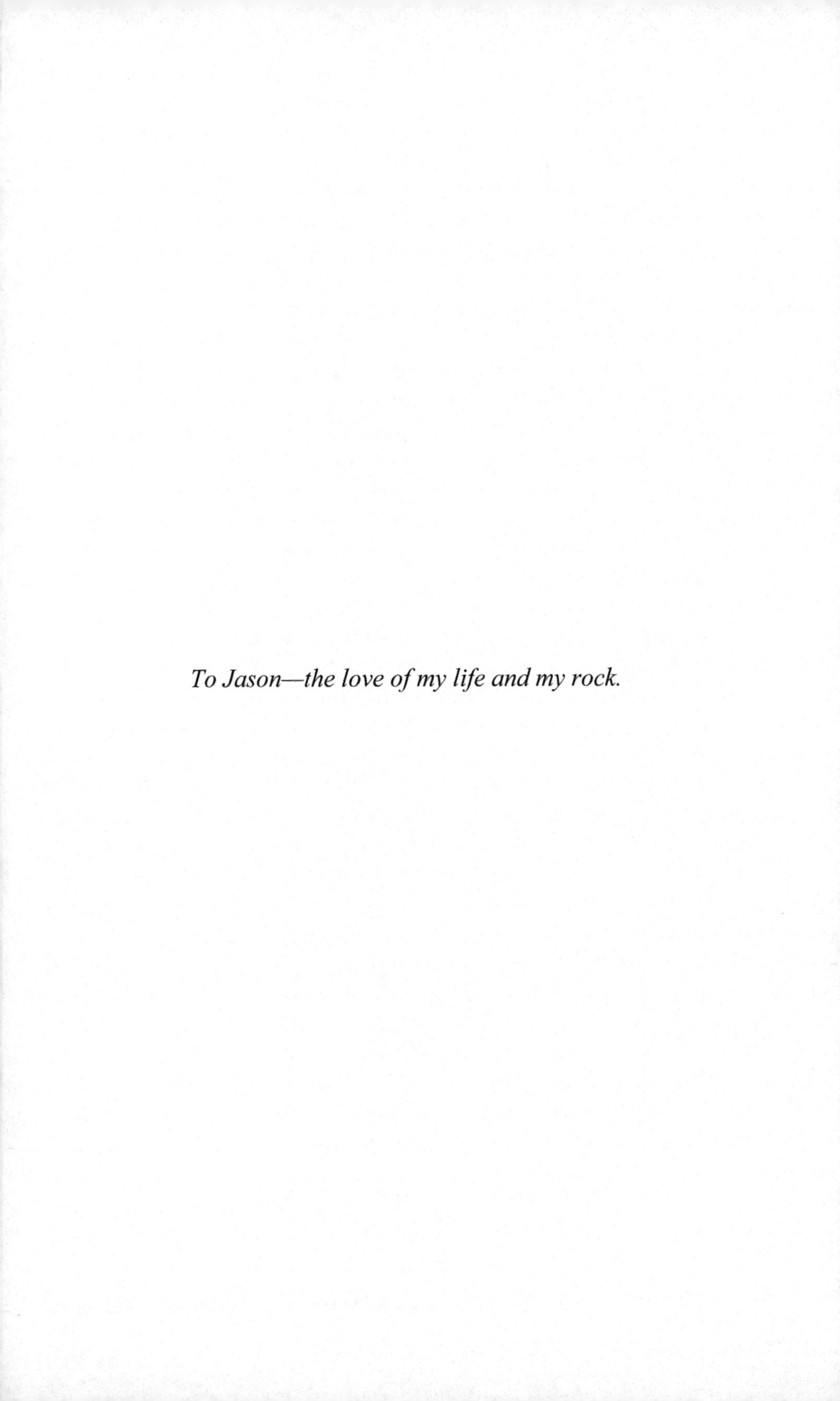

To Jason—the love of my life and my rock.

Table of Contents

Preface

Throughout grade school and into high school, I struggled academically. Math, science, and anything requiring memorization seemed almost impossible. My brain didn't work like everyone else's, and my parents worried on more than one occasion if I would even graduate.

At fifteen, I started working at a local shoe store. As an extreme introvert, the manager had a lot of work to do to teach me to sell, but fortunately, he was patient. With his guidance, I finally learned how to talk to people. Because this leader took the time to mentor instead of dismissing me, he planted the seed for what would later bloom into achievement.

At the same time, I also gained more confidence in the classroom. I graduated high school and entered college, majoring in marketing and management. I excelled by getting involved on campus and taking on leadership positions within my sorority and other groups.

Through these experiences, I realized that I enjoyed leading people. Still, it wasn't until I graduated college and took my first job as an operations manager that I understood the responsibility of being a leader. It is *hard* work!

As you may know, raising three children and working full-time, even with a supportive spouse, is often overwhelming. Despite these challenges, I went on to successfully lead teams of hundreds of people across the globe, earned my MBA, opened my consulting and coaching practice, earned my Ph.D., and then become a dean and VP in higher education.

As my career took twists and turns over the years, sometimes I came home excited, feeling like I was driving straight ahead on the road to success. Other times, however, I knew that if my career were a car, I would be towing it out of a ditch.

At one critical point when I lost my job due to downsizing, I stopped and asked myself if I even knew what success meant. But the truth was that my definition of success needed to change.

Early in my career, it was all about *me.* What could I achieve? How high could I climb the ladder? Later, I learned that real leadership was less about me and more about what I could build with a team working together. How could *we* achieve more? This mind shift from "me" to "we" was the difference maker. The most effective leadership is all about people—succeeding on your own has far less meaning.

True success is accomplished alongside other people.

Have you ever found yourself contemplating what distinguishes successful leaders from those who fail? Or questioning the meaning of achieving success?

Whether you've experienced working with exceptional leaders, wished for better ones, or have faced obstacles in your career that seemed insurmountable, this book is written for you.

It's crafted for every person who seeks to lead themselves and others to achieve what they never thought possible before. Which means it's designed for anyone brave enough to make their world a better place.

Together, we will unpack the Leaders SUCCEED together© system: a dynamic approach that redefines leadership success as a collective journey rather than a solitary climb to the top. This system is a guide for leaders striving to unlock their fullest potential by bringing out the best in those around them by leveraging the latest research and proven strategies to take your organization to the next level.

There is nothing static about leadership. It's like the framed quote that has been on my bedside table for over thirty years that says, "Success is a journey and not a destination."

Leadership is a journey, and I'm so glad you are taking control of your career and joining me as we navigate that road together.

Before we dive in together, I want to acknowledge the obvious: There are thousands of leadership authors. So why should you trust me? Because I have achieved leadership success *and* leadership failure. And, often, the deepest learnings come from our missteps and overcoming adversity.

This leadership system I created is built upon what I have discovered from research and personal experience. The Leaders SUCCEED together© system brings together some of what you may already know with proven assessments and techniques in an easy-to-follow and practical process for you and your organization.

They say you have the most impact on the world if you work on problems that break your heart. For me, those two problems are: 1. Seeing people work for bosses who make their lives miserable, and 2. Watching leaders lack the systems and support they need to live up to their potential.

My life's pursuit is fostering growth for leaders and organizations to thrive in the face of change and uncertainty to become the best they can be. So, whether you're a seasoned leader seeking to maximize your teams, a coach in search of strategies to empower your clients, or a new leader stepping into the role for the first time, this book is designed for you. The Leaders SUCCEED together© system is your blueprint for cultivating the leaders of tomorrow, today.

The first time I shared pieces of what this book would later become was one memorable evening when I was working as the founding dean of the business college in a small liberal arts university. I was asked to talk to parents and students.

How I became a dean is like many things in life and business: a winding path. I began my career in financial services, and somehow, successfully navigated through the Great Recession, landing in a marketing and consulting career.

Years earlier, however, while I was earning my undergraduate degree, our management professor described X and Y theories of motivation with a slide show. It showed someone being hit with a stick while also being prodded ahead with a carrot dangling in front of them. He explained that workplace motivation leadership Theory X requires constant prodding of employees because they are inherently lazy. While Theory Y assumes the opposite—employees are motivated to work and take on additional responsibilities when they find meaning in their roles.

As I sat there listening to him, saying that Theory X was the way to manage, something deep inside me stirred. I had been working since I was 15, and I knew he was wrong. At that time, it was disrespectful to question a professor, and for me, it was at triple the social cost, because I was afraid to ask questions. Yet, I shyly raised my hand and said, "Professor, can you please give me an example of how this worked when you were managing someone at a workplace?" He looked at me puzzled, shifted his glasses and said, "What do you mean? I have never managed anyone, but the theory says this."

At that time, I didn't understand the value that research professors bring to the management field; I now appreciate their contributions. However, right then and there, in the second row of that business college classroom, I made a promise to myself that I would go out in the world and gain at least 20 years of experience in leadership and come back to teach students what it means to be a great leader. I vowed to prove that Theory Y is more accurate than X—so that's what I did.

Back to that evening presentation.

I was asked to give the keynote address at the honorary society induction. The topic? Leadership, of course.

I opened with: "If you've ever had a bad boss, please stand up."

All two hundred people stood up except for one man. I asked the audience to sit down and then told the man, "Wow, you are really lucky! You've never had a bad boss?"

He said, "Nope! I've always worked for myself."

We all laughed.

Silently, I wondered if his employees would be standing or sitting. Then, I began my talk about leadership, beginning with self-awareness and a few of the concepts we'll discuss in this book. Afterward, members of the audience asked if I would make a video and send it to their workplaces to let their managers know how they should lead.

I smiled and played along with their suggestions, but the stories they shared about their bad bosses and the impact they had on them and their families touched me deeply.

It was becoming increasingly evident to me—we had a leadership crisis in our workplaces. I had seen the data on declining engagement. Then the post-pandemic shifts to quiet and then loud quitting. Through the classes I have taught and executives I have coached in my private consulting practice, I heard story after story of bullying coworkers, inept bosses, and toxic cultures.

I, too, had experienced these types of challenges at work. As I helped more business owners, I also realized that leadership issues were at the heart of many company failures. It's why this system is built not just for those who are embedded in corporations, but for entrepreneurs and anyone who wants to lead themselves and those around them better.

We all have the potential to be good leaders—even if it's not part of your title. As coworkers and team members, we have influence in the workplace.

People tell me frequently that they don't like their jobs. When I ask them why they stay, it's almost never about a paycheck. It's almost always about the leadership or workplace culture.

That's why the Leaders SUCCEED together© system is such a critical and time-sensitive system.

As you read this book, you will find leadership concepts that I wish I had known much earlier in my career. I will change the names and details surrounding the real stories I share to honor the privacy of the people involved.

At the end of each chapter, I will ask you to complete a Do, Reflect, and Discuss exercise because we learn best when actively reflecting and sharing with others.

Discussion guides specific to your career type and supplemental materials are available at leaderssucceedtogether.com. They will make reading the book an even more practical experience.

As you read, I only ask you to keep your mind open. Change can be uncomfortable. Take heart; we will go on this journey together to discover how to create growth-focused cultures where people can become the leaders they were meant to be.

Chapter 1: The Leaders SUCCEED together© System

Why Leadership?

Leadership is just one word. Yet, leaders have massive influence in our lives. Anyone who has ever experienced a bad boss, toxic culture, or dysfunctional workgroup can tell you that these situations do not just cause problems within their *work* lives, but their personal lives are also impacted.

For the Leadership Skeptics

Recently, a woman in my one of my leadership programs said, "I heard Steve Jobs yelled and didn't do a lot of what you talk about in your book. So why should we?"

Other skeptics have named leaders in the public eye who are exhibiting anything but self-awareness. One leader challenged me on why he needed to learn these concepts when stepping on people worked so well for others in his organization. I flipped the question.

"What kind of culture does that create?" I asked. "And is it one that's enjoyable?"

He shook his head. "No, it's terrible."

I said, "That's your answer. I'm here to inspire leaders to take a different approach and create high-performing cultures where people want to come to work."

And on the Steve Jobs question, my response is that we all know he was a brilliant innovator. However, would he have accomplished anything of greatness if he had worked alone? Definitely not. He had a team of people surrounding him. Also ... I think we can all agree Steve Jobs was one of a kind.

We all fall short as leaders. We are only able to overcome our shortcomings by working *together*.

Leaders set the tone. Taking responsibility for how we lead gives us choice and autonomy over our careers and reinforces our obligation as leaders to those around us. How we lead matters. Not only for our professional success, but to become the very best version of ourselves.

Your Leadership Legacy

How much time do you spend working? If you work full-time at 40 hours a week, that's 2,080 hours a year. Assuming you begin working at 18 and retire at 65 (many of us will work longer), you will have worked 47 years—which means 97,760 hours.

How we spend almost 98,000 hours of our lives matters!

Even if you don't have a job where you manage other people directly or are a solopreneur out on your own, you're still a leader because you lead yourself and everyone around you daily.

John Maxwell defines leadership as influence—nothing more, nothing less. You have the power to influence everyone you meet.

At work, you can toil in frustration until you retire, or you can embrace the power of leadership to become the best version of yourself and encourage those around you to do the same. This choice of how you decide to show up at work is yours. You get to make that decision every day.

The Leaders SUCCEED together© system guides and encourages you to embrace the opportunity to succeed as a leader, no matter how early or late you are in your career. Even if you consider yourself an exceptional leader, understanding the system will provide you with a process to share with others as you look to be the leader who leaves a lasting, positive legacy for those around you.

Secrets in the System

Like me, some of us begin our careers focused on success for ourselves, thinking about promotions, what we can gain from the job, and what we can achieve.

Others begin their careers not thinking about the WIFM (what's in it for me) and tirelessly focus on managing processes, procedures, and people, while never feeling like they achieved their desired success.

Success, as I define it here, is founded on relational leadership. Ask anyone who is married; good relationships take work. I will show you how to move beyond success for yourself and your organization and toward a much more meaningful life by developing a leadership style where you and everyone around you are operating at their maximum potential.

Since we influence people, which is leadership, in our personal and professional lives, the secrets to success hidden throughout this system will help you achieve what you want at work and at home—improving relationships in every aspect of your life. All you need to do is learn the system and commit to practicing it each day.

As with many things in life, leadership learning is never finished—it's ongoing. So, we must develop our skills and achieve success as we define it. I am so happy you decided to take this exciting journey along the winding path of leadership that could change your life.

Let's get started!

Leadership as an Art

Sheryl Sandberg defines leadership as "… making others better as a result of your presence and ensuring that impact lasts in your absence."

Colin Powell frames it beautifully: "Leadership is all about people … It is all about motivating people to get the job done. You must be people centered."

I resonate with these views, and my friend and leadership scholar Dr. Lisa Gick shared a definition with me that I believe to be true. She defines leadership as:

Leadership (verb): inspire and affect shared purpose, direction, and generative change through meaningful relationship-building, collaboration, and innovation in the complexity of human systems.

As a business owner or executive, think about how that applies to your clients or customers. Don't you want your impact to be developing meaningful relationships, while navigating the change and complexity of the world? It's leadership that takes your business from self-serving profit generation to making the lives of the people you serve better.

Why Focus on Leadership Now?

The number of people who have confided in me over the years about bad bosses, bullying, and toxic workplaces is staggering. Many entrepreneurs have felt pushed to start their businesses and leave their careers because they could no longer deal with office politics. Then, they find they have a new challenge ahead as they take on new and different issues in leading themselves and others as entrepreneurs.

In my professional development workshops, a frequent complaint I hear is about the generational conflicts arising because of varying views about what it means to work and succeed. Teams struggle to collaborate, communicate, and resolve conflicts, making it difficult to achieve their goals because they can't connect.

Gallup estimates that only 23% of employees worldwide and 32% in the U.S. are actively engaged at work,[1] I am confident that now is the time for this discussion.

With five generations of people in the workforce, it's time we commit to developing leaders for our future. It's time we strengthened the leadership skills and connections between our diverse team members, often distributed all over the country or globe. It's time we take a stand together and commit to learning the art of leadership amidst the ever-changing conditions we will continue to face over time.

We know leadership isn't easy, but I'm still hopeful. Because we also understand that the potential to become better leaders exists within each of us. Not perfect ones, but better, and better is good enough to change our workplace—and our world.

Management vs. Leadership

What's the difference between management and leadership?

I agree with what Admiral Grace Hopper says—you manage things, and you lead people.

While 'manager' and 'leader' are often used interchangeably, they embody distinct roles. Contextually, the word 'management' lacks empathy and trust. While management is needed as a skill for any leader, it isn't effectively applied to leading others.

Leaders, on the other hand, succeed through people, drawing out their best skills and abilities. I'll let you decide what you think about leadership versus management. But I never want to feel like I am being managed by anyone. Having a great leader or being one? I'll take that any day.

Leadership Styles

A common question I receive in my leadership development program is, "What is the best leadership style?"

While transformational, servant, and transactional styles are well-known, no single style is universally effective. I don't know about you, but it was liberating when I learned that I didn't have to change the core of who I was to be a good leader.

It was a relief—I couldn't figure out how to walk around being fake all day. Just ask anyone who knows me. They'll tell you that what you see is what you get. I'm the same person on my back patio sipping my favorite beverage as I am with clients or presenting in front of hundreds of people.

Great leaders are authentic, but there are some key behaviors and approaches that make them effective—which is where the Leaders SUCCEED together© system comes into play.

If you want to see a complete list of leadership styles that researchers have identified and the impact they have on those they lead, go to the book's website, leaderssucceedtogether.com, which has various tools you can use throughout the book.

The Leaders SUCCEED together© system

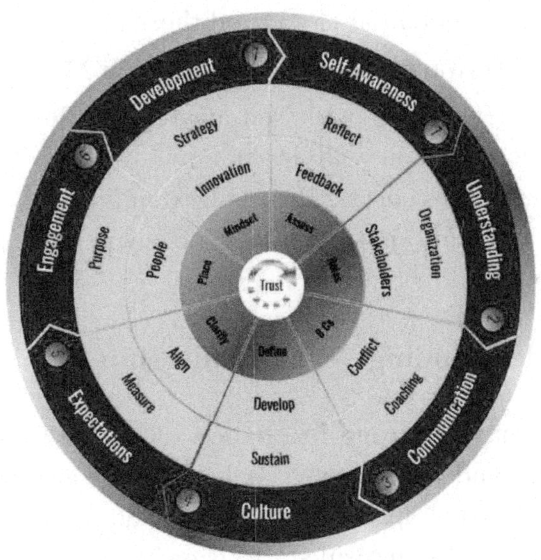

Leaders SUCCEED together© system

The Leaders SUCCEED together© system is a circular, ongoing process, symbolizing continuous development and progress. It's designed for those who aspire to make a positive impact. This system is a guide for becoming the leader you want to follow.

Although I debated calling it a model or framework versus a system, I decided that models were stagnant, and frameworks didn't give enough details to allow people to take action.

In contrast, systems are alive, interactive, and actionable. Leadership development is ongoing, active, and alive, so I have named it a system. If you call it a model, I won't correct you, but my hope in writing this book is that you will see this process you are about to learn as alive, interactive, and ongoing.

There are seven steps in the Leaders SUCCEED together© system, designed to take you and your organization to the next level and maximize the potential of you and those around you.

Step 1: Self-awareness—The Leadership Mirror

Your journey begins with self-awareness, the foundation for leadership success. You will learn how to assess yourself, seek feedback, and self-reflect. By understanding your strengths, weaknesses, and blind spots, you, and those you lead can grow more than you thought possible.

Step 2: Understanding—The Leadership Lens

Once you have a strong foundation of self-awareness, you will better understand your role, stakeholders, and the complex organizational landscape you navigate. You need the necessary knowledge to make informed decisions and build meaningful relationships inside and outside your organization. This step also reinforces the fact that taking on the responsibility for leading a team is a serious-yet-rewarding business.

Step 3: Communication—The Leadership Bridge

We know that effective communication is the cornerstone of leadership. In this step you will learn how to leverage the "8 Cs" of communication, offering guidance on conveying messages clearly and persuasively. Additionally, you will learn how to manage conflict constructively and master the art of coaching, fostering better teamwork and collaboration.

Step 4: Culture—The Leadership Soil

Since leaders set the tone, they also create the culture. By learning how to define, develop and sustain a positive work culture, you can take your organization further and play a significant role in shaping the organization's identity.

Step 5: Expectations—The Leadership Compass

Just like a ship relies on the captain to steer the boat, we rely on leaders to clarify, align, and measure expectations to ensure everyone is on the same page. By using actionable strategies for setting goals, aligning them with the organization's mission, and establishing metrics to gauge progress effectively, you will achieve the results your organization needs you to deliver.

Step 6: Engagement—The Leadership Spark

This step teaches you how to create an environment where employees feel motivated and inspired to contribute their best daily. Engagement leads to higher job satisfaction and productivity, so leaders who engage their teams focus on people, purpose and place.

Step 7: Development—The Leadership Growth Engine

Change is constant. Leaders who embrace growth mindsets, encourage innovation, and focus on designing, aligning, and executing strategy keep the system moving in the right direction.

Trust is at the system's center because trust is at the foundation of leadership—it's at the heart of the system. Everything you say and do as a leader creates or destroys trust, impacting your credibility. Staying true to ethics and integrity throughout these steps will keep you building upon this most critical foundation of leadership.

By following the Leaders SUCCEED together© system, you will develop the skills and mindset required to lead within any organization. Whether you are a seasoned leader looking to enhance your abilities or someone aspiring to take on leadership roles, this book provides a valuable roadmap for your journey to success.

Chapter Summary

We looked at various definitions of leadership focused on influencing people to achieve common goals. We differentiated between management and leadership, agreeing with Admiral Grace Hopper's quote, "You manage things; you lead people." While management is necessary, the role itself lacks the empathy and trust critical for leaders to succeed.

- **Everyone is a leader.** Leadership isn't confined to titles or positions. It's about influence—the power to shape the environment and people around us. With this power comes responsibility because leaders can influence people positively or negatively. By recognizing our role as a leader in setting the tone, we can improve both our personal and professional relationships.
- **The Leaders SUCCEED together© system.** This isn't just another leadership theory, it's a hands-on, dynamic system tailored for those who want to embrace the ongoing and never-ending leadership journey. With 7 Steps revolving around trust, we are building a better future around how we define success as we lead:
    1. **Self-Awareness—The Leadership Mirror:** Here, we embark on an inward journey. It's all about holding up a mirror to our strengths, weaknesses, and blind spots. This step is like the foundation of a skyscraper—essential for towering success. During this step in the process, we will dive deep into self-assessment, feedback, and reflection.
    2. **Understanding—The Leadership Lens:** As a leader, how well do you understand the environment required to

succeed? Are there things about your team or clients that you need to better understand? Here we learn that people are complex and part of a larger system that is designed to either bring out their best or impede their growth.

3. **Communication—The Leadership Bridge:** It isn't just about talking—communication is about connecting. We explore the "8 Cs" of impactful communication along with how to take fear out of conflict. We become masterful coaches to bring out the best in those around us.
4. **Culture—The Leadership Soil:** Here, we delve into cultivating a thriving organizational culture. Like a gardener who nurtures the soil, leaders have an opportunity to enrich cultures. I will show you how to create, maintain, and sustain a culture that reflects the vision, mission, and values you need to get everyone involved, working together to achieve success.
5. **Expectations—The Leadership Compass:** Setting and aligning expectations is crucial. This step is about charting a clear course for your team, aligning goals with the mission, and setting measurable markers for success. It's like a compass, ensuring everyone is sailing in the same direction.
6. **Engagement—The Leadership Spark:** Leaders who take the time to design their organizations around the right places, people, and purpose will benefit from an engaged team. Everyone wants to be part of something bigger than themselves and know that they have value. This step is about lighting the fire that drives higher job satisfaction and productivity.
7. **Development—The Leadership Growth Engine:** Growth is never by chance—it's the result of forces working together. This last step focuses on fostering a forward-thinking mindset, driving innovation, and preparing for the

future. It's the engine that propels both personal and organizational advancement.

At the heart of this system is trust, the cornerstone of all leadership endeavors. Trust is the glue that holds all these steps together, forming a robust and credible leadership presence.

Whether you're a seasoned leader or just starting out, the Leaders SUCCEED together© system is your roadmap toward growth, influence, and success.

Do

1. Visit leaderssucceedtogether.com to download additional materials and sign-up for our newsletter.
2. If you don't have a partner or group reading this book with you, recruit 1-5 people or join one of our groups. We learn so much from discussions with others!
3. If you do have a discussion group, schedule weekly, bi-weekly, or monthly meetings. Hold each other accountable for doing the reading and the work.

Reflect

1. What are three goals you would like to achieve by reading this book?
2. In your own words, how do you define leadership? Who are examples of great leaders? What did they do?
3. When reading the summaries of the seven steps in the system, which one do you believe is a strength you have? Which one do you think you will need to work on the most?

Discuss

1. What are your goals in reading this book? Share one or two with the group.
2. Discuss how you define leadership and create a definition of leadership as a group.
3. Talk about which of the seven steps in the Leaders SUCCEED together© system are most interesting. If you don't have a professional facilitator, identify someone to lead each of the seven steps.

Chapter 2: Self-Awareness

The Leadership Mirror

Why Self-Awareness?

I was facilitating a workshop for a company, and a man in his forties raised his hand and said, "Why should people who already have this leadership stuff locked down waste their time in this session?"

His colleagues and team members rolled their eyes and shifted in their seats uncomfortably. Obviously, he did not have this "leadership stuff locked down."

I politely said, "Well, maybe you can share your experiences with us while you're here."

Throughout the session, I could see some light bulbs going off in his mind. (That's one of the best parts of what I do!) A few weeks later I received an email from one of his team members thanking me for what I had shared. He said his boss had grown in self-awareness. He now understood how his behaviors were reducing performance on the entire team—for the very first time!

That is why I love this work so much.

Self-awareness is the ability to recognize and understand our own thoughts, emotions, and behaviors, and the potential impact these can have on ourselves and anyone around us. Increasing self-awareness has positive outcomes for entire organizations, such as leadership effectiveness, job performance, follower satisfaction, and organizational commitment.[2]

I wish I had known earlier in my career. (Just FYI, when someone describes you as a bull in a China shop, it's not a compliment.) Taking a hard look in the mirror has helped me improve my relationships personally and professionally and has guided me in making better career decisions.

I'd like to tell you it's a one-time activity, but understanding and leading yourself is a lifelong journey. Anyone who knows me would be quick to tell you that I still have work to do.

Have you ever worked with someone who lacked self-awareness? It can be painful to watch—and even more difficult if that person is your boss or someone close to you.

It's like when a coworker I knew walked into a conference room to give a big client presentation with a piece of lettuce in his teeth. Everyone was trying to ignore it, and given the situation, it wouldn't have been appropriate to interrupt him. So, we all just sat there, distracted by lettuce, and wishing he had looked in the mirror.

Lack of self-awareness is sometimes unintentional, like lettuce sticking around after lunch. Or accidental, like when my mom told me she walked on stage at a conference with her dress tucked into her pantyhose. Honestly, I'm glad she told me that story because after I heard it, I always checked myself thoroughly for no wardrobe malfunctions.

It's nice when we get to learn from others' mistakes! Other times, however, our lack of self-awareness is built around the thought that if people don't like us how we are, it's their problem. Whatever the source, when leaders lack self-awareness, it impacts everyone around them.

For instance, one night a friend called to tell me how her boss berates people during meetings. Everyone can see that these chew-out sessions—as they have been named—do nothing to improve performance. She wonders if he even realizes how belittling and demotivating his tone and words are, so they continue to lose talented people who don't want to deal with his bad behaviors.

It shouldn't be surprising that studies have found that self-awareness is also associated with various positive outcomes, such as increased well-being, better decision-making, and improved interpersonal relationships.[3]

Here are four specific reasons to invest in the continuous process of improving your self-awareness and working with others to develop theirs as well:

1. **Build better relationships.** Relationships are crucial to leadership. When leaders are aware of their emotions, thoughts, and behaviors, they are in a better position to regulate them and understand how they might affect others, which will build trust, rapport, and positivity with their followers.[4]
2. **Make better decisions.** When leaders are aware of their own biases, values, and assumptions, they are less likely to be swayed by them and more likely to make objective and rational decisions.[5]

3. **Adapt to different situations and contexts.** Self-aware leaders excel in different and demanding situations. They are more likely to bring about strategic change.[6]
4. **Avoid career derailment.** We all have blind spots that we can't see. However, self-awareness can help us be honest with ourselves and manage our behaviors in ways that reduce burnout and even unethical behavior.[7]

Two leaders who are excellent examples of high and low self-awareness are Satya Nadella, the CEO of Microsoft, and Travis Kalanick, the former CEO of Uber.

Satya Nadella is widely regarded as a leader with high self-awareness. In an interview with the Wall Street Journal, Nadella emphasized the importance of empathy and self-awareness in leadership. He also spoke about the need for leaders to be authentic and self-reflective and to recognize their own strengths and weaknesses.[8] Nadella's focus on empathy and self-awareness has driven Microsoft's cultural transformation and its renewed success in recent years.[9]

In contrast, Travis Kalanick has been criticized for his lack of self-awareness. As the founder and former CEO of Uber, Kalanick was known for his aggressive and confrontational leadership style. He was accused of creating a toxic workplace culture and was forced to resign as CEO in 2017 following a series of scandals.[10] Experts have pointed to Kalanick's lack of self-awareness as a major factor in Uber's cultural problems, and his fault and downfall as CEO.[11]

The differences between these two leaders highlight the importance of self-awareness for leaders to succeed. Self-aware leaders are more likely to build positive workplace cultures, make sound decisions, and inspire others. In contrast, leaders who lack self-awareness may be more prone to making mistakes, creating toxic environments, and ultimately damaging their organizations.

Self-Awareness and Self-Leadership

We have established that we are all leaders because we all influence people around us and must lead ourselves every day. Self-leadership, to me, is often the most challenging job. Yes, leading myself is hard work!

For instance, as I write this chapter, I am leading myself to the pantry to eat another cookie I don't need. But later, I will lead myself to the gym because I know it's good for me and those around me that I stay healthy. Self-leadership matters, and effectively leading ourselves begins with a healthy dose of self-awareness.

As individuals, we set the tone in our workplaces and within our communities. Our attitudes, conversations, and actions can influence anyone we interact with throughout the day. We will cover culture in a later chapter, but as leaders, sustaining positive work cultures starts with us. That means online as well.

Do you know anyone who doesn't practice self-leadership on social media? I have been guilty of reflecting and then taking down a post or two over the years and warning my children and students that everything in your brain doesn't need to be published to the world. Having seen both careers and brands decimated by people not leading themselves well with what they post online means that it starts with self-awareness and ends with self-leadership.

What Is Your Team Saying About You?

In one of my leadership workshops, I asked a group of managers what their employees said about them at the dinner table. They looked at me puzzled. One of them said, "Wow, I never thought about it like that. When I'm at home, I talk about the trouble my team causes me and how difficult they make my life at work. But I never considered what their dinner-table conversations about me were."

The impact of how we lead ourselves at work radiates through every aspect of our lives. If we are miserable in our jobs, we can't contain it. Misery is contagious and has the potential to affect our families, friends, and colleagues—even if we think we've mastered the poker face.

The good news is that positivity is also contagious. While being positive, we can influence people through simple acts like sharing a smile or a word of encouragement. Positivity spreads faster than negativity.

Diane Egbers, the CEO of Leadership Excelleration, says, "Positivity is professionalism." I love that quote because, in many of our workshops, you can see the dawn of realization on people's faces when it registers that being a professional means being positive. That doesn't mean not addressing problems or issues—it means exhibiting self-leadership in how you show up at work.

Ask yourself: If emotions are contagious, what am I spreading today?

This is why I began the Leaders SUCCEED together© system with self-awareness. Although it may be one of the most challenging skills to master, it's one of the most important. Within the Leaders SUCCEED together© system, the three parts of self-awareness are 1. Assess, 2. Feedback, and 3. Reflect.

Using these three steps will support your growth as a leader who wants to succeed—not just for themselves, but for everyone around them.

Let's look at each closely.

1. Assess

Some of my most challenging coaching clients think they have it all figured out. At the same time, everyone around them can see that they are sabotaging their own success by not realizing they have certain behaviors holding them back.

I've found that the most insight and growth come when we use a variety of assessments to understand ourselves better. Just like you need to know your current location to map a route, assessment gives us insight into our current location as a leader.

The great news is that we're all different. Each person has a unique DNA. (I mean, how boring would it be if we were all wired the same?) But this also means that we each use a very different pair of 'lenses' to view the world.

To better understand ourselves and one another, assessing our personality styles, strengths, emotional intelligence, and values can be a great start to increasing self-awareness. Fortunately, there are several assessments you can use that have been cross-culturally validated.

Let's look at a few together.

- **Personality Styles.** We've all heard the nature-versus-nurture debate about how our personalities are formed. Most researchers have settled on a combination of genetics and experiences. From a communication and work-style perspective, we also have distinct differences. A few tools to assess your personality and workstyle to improve self-awareness are Meyers Briggs, DiSC, and Enneagram.
- **Strengths.** Research finds that people are much more effective at building upon their strengths than spending most of their time fixing their weaknesses. I wish I had learned that fact earlier in my career when I wasted time thinking I had to be good at everything. Now, I focus on my strengths and allow people with different strengths to use theirs to benefit everyone. The best

assessments to measure strengths are Gallup StrengthsFinder, VIA Character Strengths, and Working Genius.

- **Emotional Intelligence.** Daniel Goleman and his colleagues developed the concept of emotional intelligence to understand why people with the highest IQ didn't always get ahead. Their research found that emotional intelligence (EI) was a determining factor. Emotional intelligence as a competency model for leaders is comprised of four areas: self-awareness, self-management, social awareness, and relationship management, which translates into on-the-job success.[12] Although I have found that a 360-feedback tool is one of the best ways to assess EI, there's also Emotional Quotient Inventory (EQ-i), Mayer-Salovey-Caruso Emotional Intelligence Test (MSCEIT), or an assessment within the book *Emotional Intelligence 2.0* by Travis Bradberry, Jean Greaves, and Tom Parks.
- **Values.** I can't say enough about how knowing your values increases self-awareness. Sunnie Giles surveyed global leaders to rate the top qualities of a leader, and strong ethics and integrity were number one.[13] Anyone who has ever worked in an organization with ethical lapses by leaders knows the damage they can cause. Those who have worked with high-integrity leaders know how it builds trust for internal and external customers. There are online assessments, paper exercises, and card sorts to identify your core values. There is also a free test to measure these values at Human Values Test (idrlabs.com).
- **Cloverleaf.** There is also a coaching and assessment platform that combines many of the assessments with ongoing coaching and the opportunity for organizations to create a coaching culture where team members are more self-aware. You can find more information about this system at cloverleaf.me.

Assessing ourselves can feel uncomfortable, but just like the trainer at my gym says, sometimes you must push through a little pain to get the results you want. When we learn new information about ourselves and, even more importantly, share some of our style preferences and strengths with people we work with, we build stronger and more trusting relationships.

2. Feedback

I was recently teaching in a professional development program, and I asked a class of over 30 professionals if they liked receiving feedback. Only one brave soul raised his hand. I could see from the others' body language and facial expressions that they were embarrassed they hadn't raised their hands. Everyone likes receiving feedback, right? Not so.

I asked the one who raised his hand why he enjoyed receiving feedback, and he said it helped him grow. He was right! When I asked some of those who didn't raise their hands, they shared that they didn't see the value in the feedback they typically received or feared it would be negative. Others also explained that the way previous bosses had given them feedback left them feeling upset and ineffective, so why would they want to go through that again?

One woman in the class told a story about a boss who gave her feedback that her work wasn't being completed on time when she had proof that she had met every deadline. Unfortunately, this lack of validity occurs because we're all biased when we provide feedback, and many leaders are not great at coaching. Regrettably, the fear of not wanting to hear negative feedback may prevent us from becoming the best leader we can be.

Here are several effective ways to gain feedback to improve self-awareness:

- **Performance Reviews.** Like the feedback question, most people would rather sit through a root canal than a yearly performance review. That's why many companies are eliminating them and focusing more on ongoing coaching. However, the information shared during these reviews can be invaluable for employees if they reflect on trends over time and ask the right questions.

- **360-Degree Assessments.** The Center for Creative Leadership (CCL) has created an assessment of leadership competencies. You might consider taking their CCL to learn more about how your boss, peers, and direct reports perceive you. A 360-degree assessment sends surveys to people within your organization and rates you across leadership competencies. These are most effective at helping leaders understand any blind spots they want to address.
- **Stakeholder Interviews.** Surveys provide one aspect of information, but as a consultant and coach, I find that talking with (interviewing) people is one of the best ways to get the clearest picture of what's happening within organizations. I love it because it's like putting together pieces of a puzzle. It might be uncomfortable for leaders to have someone interview people about their leadership style. However, if you have the right person to gather data and extrapolate the key themes, you'll find more value than you ever dreamed possible. This process works best using a trained outside coach or consultant. It can be expensive, so it tends to be reserved for key executives in many organizations. If you do find yourself in a position to purchase this type of valuable assessment, take advantage of it! For small businesses and startups, your personal brand is often critical for success, so you would be well-advised to conduct surveys and interviews about the level of service you provide, which you may be able to turn into testimonials later.
- **One-on-Ones or Coaching.** Many one-on-ones with managers are updates and not coaching sessions. However, you can also get solid feedback based on any meeting you have with your manager, peers, or clients. Keep track of key points and questions

they ask and how they respond to you. There is feedback hidden inside. When you receive coaching or feedback from one of your team members, vendors, or clients, ask questions and collect valuable information. If you have team members, vendors, or clients quitting around you, this is also a trend to consider. Again, not all feedback is accurate or valid, but note what information you have gathered about what you are doing well and where you may need to improve.

- **Debriefing Meetings.** Another wonderful way to gather feedback is by asking questions and listening after meetings. For example, ask open-ended questions like, "How do you think that meeting went?" or "In what ways do you think I can improve my communication?" or "What else can I do to do a better job in those meetings to support our goals?" These questions are critical to building relationships and adding to your self-awareness.
- **Active Listening.** Have you ever misunderstood someone because you were thinking about how you would respond to them instead of listening? This often happens when I'm focused on myself more than trying to understand the person I'm talking with. Active listening means being 100% present, not interrupting, and asking questions. Warning: this doesn't mean defensive interrogation when people give you feedback. Listening without judging or thinking about what you will say back is important in hearing what is being said and unsaid. It takes practice to commit to listening more actively. But when we do, we can gain important insights to improve self-awareness.
- **Truth-Tellers.** Throughout my career, I've been blessed with truth-tellers. These are mentors, peers, and even direct reports with whom I have such a strong relationship, they respectfully and honestly tell me the truth. Finding these people throughout your career is essential because they are the ones who will tell

you if you made a mistake, if someone is upset with you, or if you need to make a change. Build strong relationships and find a few people you can trust to answer tough questions.

One person I could always count on was a VP named Jared who worked for me. With a lighthearted tone, he would call or come by my office and say, "Hey, I think this person or that person may have taken what you said the wrong way."

For example, once when I spoke with the person Jared mentioned, she said, "I thought I was being fired after that meeting. When you said there were going to be organizational changes, and then you didn't approve the requisition I sent to you, I thought my department was being eliminated." How her mind took her there, I don't know. But the point is that if Jared had not called and told me to check in with her, I might have lost a talented team member due to miscommunication. Thanks, Jared!

- **Record Meetings/Presentations.** Another effective way to improve self-awareness is watching yourself in a meeting or giving a presentation. Professional speakers and athletes constantly review their recordings. When my son played football, every Saturday morning was dedicated to watching films. It's how they identified where they needed to improve on the field.

  Likewise, ask for permission to record a few meetings and review your presentations when possible. Please don't tell people that you're recording yourself for development. That might sound weird. However, it's common now to record online meetings to capture notes, and in-person meeting recordings could be used to help the entire team determine if there are ways they can improve their communication. I find it painful to watch a recording of myself, but it's worth it if you want to improve.

- **Feedback Is a Gift.** When I first heard the saying, "Feedback is a gift," I almost spit out the coffee I was drinking. My personal experience with feedback has not been great over the years. I also have a personality style that takes criticism harshly. Yet, each time I receive feedback, it provides another data point and trail marker to add to my self-awareness journey. Sure, some feedback may not be valid or fair, but over time, when you recognize the patterns, that is where your growth as a leader happens.

That brings us to the next step of self-awareness, which is taking time for reflection.

3. Reflect

Many of us run through life so quickly that we barely slow down to eat, rolling through the drive through. Think about how many things you try to do simultaneously, and how we are often admired for multitasking. One of the reasons professional coaching has exploded over the past few years is because it gives people dedicated time and space to reflect on how and what they are saying and doing.

Think about it. When was the last time someone really listened and asked you questions as you reflected upon a situation? Reflection is often neglected until something big happens—a job loss, failed project, or even divorce. These events force us to stop and think about our actions and how we ended up at the end of that road.

Once you have assessed yourself and gained feedback, one of the most powerful tools for growth as a leader who wants to succeed is reflection. Research has found that reflection is a core skill for leaders to develop.[14] It's through taking time to reflect that we come to our most significant breakthroughs. Outside of reflecting on the questions I pose in each chapter, here are some additional ways you can practice reflecting as a core skill to build self-awareness:

- **The Consultant.** I find this especially helpful during a meeting when I'm frustrated. I mentally take myself out of the meeting and pretend to observe it from above or in an empty chair. I pretend I'm a consultant who is not attached or directly connected to the outcome of the discussion. Think about the situation—not as someone on the team but as an outsider. How do you see it differently? What questions should you be asking? Depersonalizing the situation by taking yourself out of the equation and making unbiased assessments can improve your self-awareness and make you more innovative in solving problems.
- **Journaling.** I have friends who say journaling changed their lives. This can be physically writing with pen and paper or typing a note on your phone or online. I love notebooks, and rather than commit to an ongoing journal, I write recaps and notes after meetings, which helps me process the information. If you focus on what went well and what didn't in various meetings, you can discover patterns in how you act, feel, or what you do. Writing and reflecting on key questions will also bring answers you never thought possible to the surface.
- **Conversations.** Reflect on conversations at work. How much time do you spend talking about yourself versus other people? Do you gossip or talk negatively, or are you upbeat? Are people drawn to your positive energy, or do they close their door when they see you coming? I often ask the leadership classes I teach these questions, "Do the lights turns on or off when you walk into a room?" Or, said another way, "Are people happy to see you coming or going?" Reflecting upon these questions can help deepen our self-awareness and allow us to lead ourselves differently.
- **One-on-Ones or Coaching.** Reflect on the one-on-ones or coaching conversations you've had over the years, both where

you have coached others and when others have coached you. What have you learned about yourself?

- **Prayer and Mediation.** Those of you who have these practices in place know their transformational power. Taking time out of my day to pray and reflect has changed my life. Even if you're not spiritual, you can still dedicate time in the morning or evening to sit and reflect. You will be amazed by the impact and calmness reflection will bring into your life.
- **Your Last Interaction.** Take a moment to think about the last interaction you had with someone. What did they say? How did they say it? What did you say, and how did you say it? What was happening around you? How do you think they felt after the conversation ended? How did you feel? What if that were the very last interaction you ever have with that person? Did you leave the conversation in a way that demonstrated you cared about them? Or are you waiting until their funeral to tell them what they really mean to you? I know this sounds harsh and morbid, but it's within this type of stark reality that we recognize we all have an expiration date. We also have a wonderful gift called the *present.* Stopping to reflect throughout your day and week will improve your self-awareness and relationships, setting you on the path to becoming the leader you were meant to be.
- **Some Things You Can't Change.** We know that personal assessments and feedback are powerful tools that can help us develop greater self-awareness and identify areas for improvement we can work on to achieve our goals. By actively seeking feedback and being open to constructive criticism, we can accelerate our personal and professional growth and enhance our relationships through self-awareness. However, sometimes, even though we have gained feedback as part of the self-awareness puzzle, we can't seem to change. I share this because,

over the years, I have learned I have two choices: I can work around it, or I can embrace it. Here are two examples:

- **Work Around It.** I began working for a bank in a management trainee program after graduating from college. I could lead projects and manage departments, which helped me learn at a pace I never expected. One day after a meeting, my boss, a tough and wonderful mentor, said, "I can see everything you are thinking on your face. You need to fix that face." Twenty-five years later, I still can't fix my face. I have succeeded in broadening my skills and experience, but my family often teases me about my strange facial expressions. If we are at a restaurant, they can tell immediately if I don't like my food without me saying a word. Just like they won a game show, they point and say, "Mom doesn't like her food!" Professionally, I work around it by looking down and taking notes when my face is not cooperating. Unfortunately, when I'm thinking about something negative that is unrelated to where I am, I have also been chastised for having a nasty look on my face. One time a colleague accused me of giving her a "vulture face" in a meeting when I had been thinking about something unrelated. That was hurtful-but-valid feedback. I wouldn't have had an issue with my face if I'd been present mentally at the meeting. My strange facial expressions are something I don't think I'll ever be able to fix. I do my best to work around them, accept them, and make jokes when possible. It just shows that I'm human and still a work in progress.
- **Embrace It.** I hate dealing with detailed project plans. I am very detail-oriented, but having to create a project plan and monitor everyone's inputs and outputs is something I dread more than a visit to the dentist, which is one of my least favorite appointments. Early in my career, I received feedback that I needed to improve my project management skills, so I took

classes, watched videos, and downloaded software, but I still couldn't bring myself to keep the plans I made. So, I asked myself two questions: 1. Is this aligned with my strengths? 2. Do I have to do this? No. Then why was I trying? I embraced the fact that I don't enjoy managing projects, and now I always have a project manager supporting me on my consulting projects. When I worked in the corporate world, I hired people with excellent project management skills. I used to believe I had to be good at everything to be a leader. By doing that, I was robbing those around me of the opportunity to work in their strength zone. Delegating is a gift we give as we leverage the strengths of those around us. When we embrace our limitations, we also let other people shine and reinforce to ourselves that it's ok to be you.

The key reminder here is that you are the captain of your ship, and you have the choice as to what you change and what stays the same!

Chapter Summary

This chapter sets the stage for the first step in the Leaders SUCCEED together© system where we begin to get honest with ourselves about who we are and who we want to become through self-awareness. The role of self-awareness is to shape empathetic and impactful leaders. Picture it as a mirror, not just reflecting who you are, but also how you show up as a unique individual with special gifts and talents to offer the world.

- **Unveiling the Power of Self-Awareness.** You can leverage the power of self-awareness to become the leader you were meant to be.
- **The Unseen Influence.** Imagine a leader who yells at everyone in the office and thinks they are motivating people to get results. Then, their most talented team members leave, and they have no

idea why. That's the world of leaders lacking self-awareness, who can have serious, unintended impacts. Without self-awareness, leaders are like ships adrift, unaware of the waves they create.

- **Self-awareness Is a Superpower.** Self-awareness isn't just nice to have, it's a leadership superpower. It's the secret sauce for building stronger relationships, making smarter decisions, and steering through the ever-changing business landscape. It's the antidote to career stagnation and transforming good leaders into great ones.
- **A Tale of Two Leaders.** Enter Satya Nadella and Travis Kalanick—examples of high and low self-awareness. Nadella's empathetic, reflective style is contrasted with Kalanick's aggressive approach, painting a compelling picture of why self-awareness matters.
- **The Self-Awareness Trifecta.** The chapter breaks down the self-awareness step within the Leaders SUCCEED together© system into three additional transformative steps:
    1. **Assess—Your Treasure Map to Self-discovery.** Delve into a variety of assessments, from personality tests to emotional intelligence scales. It's like having a GPS for your leadership journey, helping you pinpoint where you are and where you need to go.
    2. **Feedback—The Gift that Keeps on Giving.** Sure, feedback can sting, but it's gold for growth. Embracing feedback in all forms—from formal reviews to candid chats with 'Truth-Tellers.' It's about turning every piece of feedback into a steppingstone towards greatness.
    3. **Reflect—The Power Pause: Slow Down, Breathe, and Reflect.** The art of reflection is a vital tool for self-awareness. Journal your thoughts, actively listen, engage in soul-searching conversations, meditate, and pray. It's like having a heart-to-heart with your inner leader.

- **Embrace and Adapt.** Got quirks? Own them! Learn to work around or embrace your limitations with open arms. It's about playing to your strengths and bringing your authentic self to the leadership table, while letting those around you shine.
- **The Ripple Effect.** Self-awareness isn't just about you. It's about your impact on everyone around you, from your team to your family and even the wider community. Your journey to self-awareness isn't a solo trip; it's a voyage that touches many shores.

In sum, self-awareness is the first step in the Leaders SUCCEED together© system and an invitation to embark on the most impactful place to go—the journey within. It's about unlocking the potential within you and shining your light on those around you. So, let's take off the filter and grab that real leadership mirror to see the leader you truly are—and the one you're destined to become!

Now, let's Do, Reflect, and Discuss.

Do

1. Complete 2-3 of the personality and values assessments described within the chapter. You can also access helpful links and tools at leaderssucceedtogether.com.
2. Select one of the recommended methods to gain feedback and write down a summary of the feedback you have received.
3. Practice the two ways of reflecting discussed in the chapter: the consultant and journaling technique.

Reflect

1. What surprised you about the assessments? What confirmed what you already knew about yourself?

2. What patterns have you found in the feedback you have received over time?
3. Based on what you pulled together from all the self-assessments, create a list with two columns: one, "Who Am I Today," and the other, "Who Do I Want to Become?" On the back of my business card, I ask a question: What will you do today that will help you grow toward what you want to become tomorrow? List characteristics, titles, traits, and anything else that will help you define the vision for your future self. This exercise effectively achieves transformation when you become clear about who you are now and who you want to become.

Discuss

1. Reintroduce yourself to the group based on what you discovered in the chapter. What are your strengths, core values, and personality styles? What did you know, and what surprised you?
2. How would people around you describe you as a leader? Remember, being a leader doesn't have to mean positional authority—it's all about influence. How would people say you influence them?
3. Share your vision for the leader you want to become with the group.

Chapter 3: Understanding

The Leadership Lens

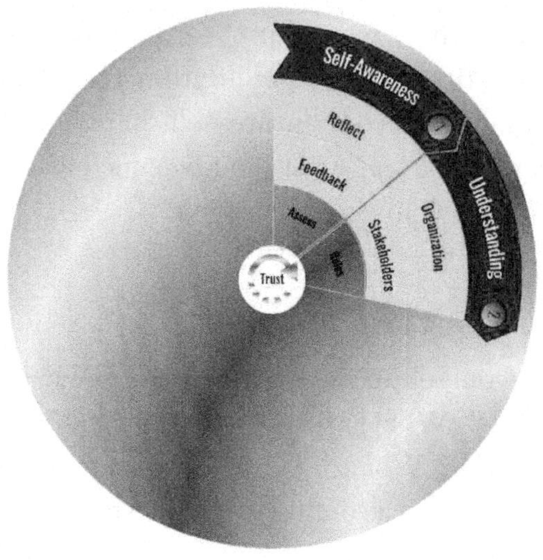

Stephen Covey said, "Seek first to understand, then to be understood." This quote has such depth that it stands the test of time. Even if we don't wear contacts or glasses, we all come to every situation wearing a unique set of lenses. How each person sees the world is unique and stems from our DNA and from each experience we have.

Embedded within each of us are silent stories. These are life changing experiences that influence how we view situations and what we believe about ourselves. I'll share one of mine here—one I have never shared publicly before.

Growing up I was a pudgy, freckled-faced girl who was painfully shy. In grade school my name was called on the intercom once a week to go to the special needs room. It was only to work on my balance, but the kids in the class thought I had a mental disability, which was made obvious by how they held their hands over their mouths, "covering" their laugher when I left the classroom.

My parents were hardworking and did everything they could to make a great life for my three siblings and me. It's always funny to hear my mom talk about living in a garage with another couple when my dad came back from serving in Vietnam. She says she was so in love; she didn't realize it was a garage. My dad began a job that turned into a lifetime career as a machinist, and my mom became a real estate agent to pay for her nursing school. She went on to work as an RN and, eventually, as a nurse practitioner.

Having been bullied relentlessly in grade school, I learned that being invisible was the best strategy. Although my family would tell you I was outspoken at home, at school I was extremely reserved.

When you grow up with multiple siblings, you try to differentiate yourself to get attention. So, one sister was known as the smart one, the other was the joyful one, my brother was the youngest and known as the goof-off … and I was the *difficult* one.

We all have successful careers now, so none of those titles matter. But in hindsight, I see that I earned my moniker by questioning everything—which has come in handy in my career.

Following our parents' example, hard work was just what we knew. But I struggled in school, even when I worked hard. When they'd line us up to recite spelling words in front of the class every Friday, my knees shook because I knew I'd always be the one out first. In math, when we had to stand at the blackboard to demonstrate a math problem, I would ask to go to the nurse because I was sick—which was true. I felt like I was going to throw up at any moment. The nurse and I became good friends during those math class periods.

One day during math class I asked the teacher to go to the nurse and she asked why. I whispered in her ear that I had diarrhea—also true. I had been sick all day knowing we had to go to the board to demonstrate our math homework. This is where spelling and math collided.

She said I could go, but only if I could spell the word *diarrhea*. When I whispered that I couldn't, she looked up and asked the entire class if they could spell it for me so I could go to the nurse. I was mortified, and everyone in the class laughed hysterically. A smart girl in the front of the class raised her hand and spelled it as the teacher wrote it on the hall pass. I went to the nurse, where I sat crying until my mom came to pick me up.

I never told my mother that story because I knew that she would walk right back in the school and give the teacher and principal a piece of her mind. The experience reinforced that I wasn't the smart one and would never be good enough. But it also told me that I had to work even harder.

When letters and numbers came together in Algebra, my mom had to go get my assignments from school every week, and my dad or my boyfriend helped me do the work. If not, I wouldn't have passed. In college I eventually figured out that I could be successful writing and using Excel. This finding built up my confidence enough to lean into my presentation skills.

Unfortunately, I still can't memorize the spelling of words, writing rules, or math computations. I thank God for computers and my editor for this book! However, the small voice of the little girl standing in the front of the classroom still shows up in my mind saying, "You are not smart enough. You are not good enough." Through hundreds of interviews in my research and with clients, I have found that I am not alone. Many of us spend our entire lives trying to prove the little voice in our minds right or wrong.

I'm sure you have silent stories of your own. Maybe have endured horrific experiences in your life, much more than bullying in grade school, and you have come out looking unscathed. Or maybe your silent stories have created behaviors in you that are driving you to success or derailing your career.

These are personal stories you never have to share with anyone. Just recognize that they are still part of who you are and remember that everyone you meet has their own silent stories we may never understand. Yet, we do have the ability to try to walk in someone's shoes, and it's a great skill for leaders. Empathy is one of the most essential skills for leadership.[15] Let's learn a little about empathy before seeking to understand the lenses others wear.

Empathy

Empathy is the ability to understand and share the feelings of others. It is the capacity to recognize, understand, and respond to their emotions and experiences, demonstrating an authentic concern for their well-being and perspectives. From a leadership perspective, empathy allows us to connect with our team members by:

- **Building Trust.** Empathy helps us build trust with our team members by creating an environment where people feel valued and understood. When leaders genuinely listen to and acknowledge their team's emotions and concerns, it fosters a sense of psychological safety and encourages open communication.[16] Trust is at the heart of the Leaders SUCCEED together© system, so you can see why empathy is part of understanding.
- **Effectively Communicating.** Empathetic leaders actively listen to their team members, seeking to understand their thoughts, feelings, and perspectives. By demonstrating genuine interest and compassion, we can establish more transparent lines of

communication, enhance collaboration, and address conflicts more effectively.[17]

- **Engaging Team Members.** Empathy contributes to higher levels of employee engagement. When we empathize with our team members, we create an inclusive and supportive work environment that promotes individual well-being and job satisfaction. Empathetic leaders foster a sense of belonging, motivation, and commitment among their team members.[18]
- **Resolving Issues and Improving Performance.** Empathy also enables leaders to identify and address underlying issues affecting their team's performance. By understanding the challenges and concerns faced by those we rely upon at work, we can provide appropriate support, guidance, and resources, leading to improved individual and team performance.

Empathy as a Strength

In one of my MBA classes, I asked if anyone found something interesting in their Gallup Strengths results. A woman in her late forties answered with tears in her eyes. She said, "All of these years my manager has been telling me that I could never be a leader because I'm too empathic. And now, I see it as a strength."

I was thrilled by her realization. My excitement quickly turned to sadness, however, when she said she never applied for leadership roles because of what one manager told her. Sure, we can become too emotionally involved in the lives of our team members. Which, after she shared more details, was clearly her case. However, empathy is a beautiful strength for leaders, and we all need to demonstrate it.

Learning Empathy

Often people ask me if empathy can be learned. Fortunately, the research says yes. Outside of a few severe psychological disorders, anyone can learn to practice empathy. Stepping into someone else's shoes and viewing the world through their lenses improves relationships on many levels and helps us understand behaviors that we may otherwise attribute to something else entirely.

For instance, I had a leader who was constantly late, so I assumed he wasn't taking his job seriously. However, when I asked him how he was doing one day, he shared that his spouse had been diagnosed with a debilitating illness. He was now responsible for caring for her and the children every morning, which made having a standard arrival time difficult.

Because he was doing project work that didn't require him to be on-site for specific coverage time in the morning, I was able to work with him on a flexible schedule that met his needs. He was so relieved and became one of our most loyal team members.

Had I not asked how he was doing and demonstrated empathy, he would have been fired or quit. Neither of which would have been good for his family, our team, or the organization.

Empathy Fatigue and Performance

Leaders may get empathy fatigue when they get too attached to the personal issues of their team members. Although I applaud them for their care and compassion, we do need to set boundaries to protect our mental health. In these cases, I recommend leaders take a step back to ensure they aren't becoming overly involved in the personal lives of their team. You can demonstrate empathy without becoming so emotionally involved that it leaves you drained, with no energy for anyone else.

Remember, we are here to help people become the best version of themselves, but if they can't do the job they were hired to do, they may need to take a leave or be invited to find a role that is a better fit for them—even if it's outside of the organization.

Managing performance is not a lack of empathy. Of course, I always hate terminating employees or business relationships. Still, sometimes it's necessary when they can't do the job.

Being empathetic and managing performance *can* coexist. We are better leaders when we care about people and hold them accountable.

Practicing Empathy

When I began talking about empathy during a professional development program, I could see a man in the middle row become uncomfortable, shifting in his seat. At one point I asked if there were questions. He said, "Can I just fake some empathy, because I can't bring myself to care about these people and their problems?"

Everyone laughed, but I knew his sentiment was on the minds of a few others. I shared with him that people value transparency in their leaders, so "faking it until you make it" can be a risky strategy.

However, empathy is not about being emotionally involved. It's about understanding their perspective, so practicing—not faking—empathy is fine. Even if you don't feel it down in your soul, you can still practice empathy by acknowledging their feelings and situations without getting overly involved emotionally. Demonstrating care for your people is something every leader needs to do if they want to make a lasting, positive impact. So, if you really don't care about people, it's best to avoid leadership roles at work.

Now that I have shared the importance of empathy, let's discuss the three aspects of understanding that you can focus on to succeed as a leader in the Leaders SUCCEED together© system. These are 1. Role, 2. Stakeholders, and 3. Organization. By following the Leaders SUCCEED together© system to increase your understanding, you will be on your way to continuous development in becoming the leader you were meant to be.

1. Role

Sometimes, people take on a new leadership role and run in like the place is on fire and their job is to put it out. Sadly, I've done this a few times throughout my career. Often, you can clean up the mess and start fresh with some changes to your leadership approach, while in other situations, you should move on because you've damaged too many relationships.

As I spent time reflecting on my own behaviors over the years, I wondered why I engaged in this type of self-sabotage when I knew better. I realized that my zest to achieve success pushed me to ignore almost everything in this book that I'm now sharing that would have helped me succeed.

From a career perspective, some of the roles I've taken involved what I like to call dumpster fires. These are serious challenges that must be solved using creativity and speed. I also love to build things, so I want new and innovative roles as I believe I can succeed in those.

Many of my leaders have said, "You will run through a brick wall to get things done." It wasn't until later in my career that I realized this rush to succeed without understanding myself, the organization, and those around me backfired often, leaving a relational mess. Sure, maybe my career progressed a lot faster than others', but there is a less-destructive way.

Beginning with self-awareness and moving through this Leaders SUCCEED together© system has helped leaders succeed AND maintain better relationships. Allowing everyone around us to use their strengths improves outcomes and work environments.

Studies have found that up to 60% of new leaders (even executives) fail within the first 24 months.[19] Many of the reasons cited revolve around the inability to integrate themselves into the company culture and communicate effectively, which we will cover in the following chapters. However, this process begins with understanding your role, how you fit within the organization, the key stakeholders, and how the organization makes money.

From a role perspective, here are a few areas to clarify, even if you have been in your leadership position for a while:

- **Job Description.** Sometimes, I have clients who take on a leadership role without a job description, which rarely turns out well. For instance, I received a phone call from a friend who had been placed in a new role. She was being called the sales support manager by the CEO but took the job without a job description. There was also little communication with the rest of the organization about what she was supposed to be doing, so people had their ideas about how this role should support them. These people began complaining to the CEO about her not doing what they thought she should when it wasn't the job she and the CEO discussed. Her experience reinforces why you should always review an updated job description for your role. Just expect that not everything you will do will be on there. In most high-performing organizations, you will always be asked to do more. However, at a minimum, ensure you are accomplishing the role you were hired to do. If you are a business owner or founder, it's still wise to write out your job description to keep you in your areas of strength. This description will also help you identify where you need to hire for support.
- **Goals.** The second aspect of your role as a leader is to verify that you have written goals to accomplish. Even if the company doesn't require monthly, quarterly, or yearly goals, set them up for yourself. If you're an entrepreneur, this action is critical because you won't have anyone else holding you accountable. Daily, weekly, monthly, and yearly goal setting will inform your

focus and effort as well as give you a sense of accountability and accomplishment. If you're in a company still doing yearly reviews, this will also make your year-end self-evaluations easy because you've tracked and documented your achievements.

- **Knowledge and Connection Mapping.** From a role perspective, knowing what connections you need to rely on internally and externally is critical for leaders. Mapping out any additional knowledge or skills you will need to enhance your role will set you up for success. We'll talk about stakeholders next—this is about mapping out where your time is best spent connecting to the right people, meetings, and learning opportunities for your role.
  Once you have reviewed your job description and understand your goals, laying out a plan to ensure you've made all the needed connections and have all the required skills to achieve your goals will help determine if there are areas of deficiency. Sometimes, clients in this phase overlook a fundamental connection or skill they need to succeed, and it derails their career. We know that success doesn't happen alone. We need to work together with those around us. Take a break, go for a walk, meditate, pray, or do whatever works for you to open your mind to all the possibilities for the connections, knowledge, and skills you need to succeed.

Once you've clearly understood your role by gaining clarity and mapped out the essential connections and knowledge you will need to succeed, the next area to focus on within the Leaders SUCCEED together© system is confirming you understand the key stakeholders you will need to build relationships with and influence to achieve success as a leader.

2. Stakeholders

Stakeholders are people—the people who have a stake in your success and the success of your organization. The ones I like to focus on understanding the most are your team, peers, boss, and clients/customers. If you're an entrepreneur, you may not have a direct boss but a board of directors. If you're a solopreneur, you may not have a team. Yet, everyone has stakeholders.

The key to mapping out your stakeholders is to ask yourself who has a stake in your success. Who are the people expecting results from you, you serve, or rely on to deliver on the promises you make?

Your Team

If you have a team, it's one of the most important areas to focus on understanding. I know a leader who recently took over a new division, and he skipped this step of understanding and went right to telling everyone what he thought they should do. Unfortunately, the results were disastrous—he lost the majority of his talented team because he didn't care about the value they brought to the organization. He showed no interest in the work they had done to make their division one of the highest performing in the company.

Other leaders have shared that they have taken over poorly performing departments and didn't take enough time to understand their teams, leading them to make incorrect decisions that could have been avoided. Even if you've been leading the same team for years, taking time to understand what is happening within the team and between the team members pays off.

Here are a few areas to focus on with your team:

- **Conversation.** Understanding those team members who report to you is a top priority. Even if you're a C-level executive, get down to the lowest level of the organization to connect with some of the people. In every role I've taken on, I have scheduled listening-only one-on-ones the first week in my position. I share a little about myself, but the main objective is simply listening to people.

Below are a few questions:

- ✓ Tell me about yourself. How long have you been here, where did you go to school, are you from the local area? What do you enjoy outside of work? Take note of whatever personal information they are willing to share about their family. (For some people, it may feel intrusive to share too much information, so don't push like it's an interrogation. For others, you might hear everything. This will also give you insight into their communication style.)
- ✓ What do you enjoy most about your job? What do you enjoy most about working here? (Figure out what each person enjoys most about their work.)
- ✓ Do you have any ideas about what we might need to do to improve? (This is critical because it will help you understand what's important to them, and it will also allow you to make changes based on feedback, allowing you to give credit to people for good ideas you implement.)

- **Observation.** Observations about your team members and how they interact with one another, you, and outside stakeholders are powerful. Even if you have known these individuals for years, observing how they interact and conduct themselves with you as their leader is worth the time and effort.
  Here are some methods of observation: View or witness communications between team members, read emails, and attend meetings virtually or in person. For remote work, much of your observations will be virtual, which is also an effective way to understand those who work with you and the team dynamics at play.

- **Team Development.** Investing in team development is an area where leaders find significant payback. I frequently do workshops with teams, and you can see within hours how everyone contributes and where they need to grow.

  A leader recently asked me to conduct a self-awareness workshop with their team. Afterward, he said he couldn't believe how much he learned about how the team works together well (and not-so-well) just by participating in a development session with them. Group coaching sessions also work well for understanding how teams can collaborate and reduce conflict.

  Some leaders do these once and never again. However, group dynamics change with time, and adding a new person will impact the entire team. Investing in ways your team can develop together outside of working on work will deepen connections and your understanding of how to bring out the best in each person.

Your Peers

An often-overlooked fact? Your peers can make or break your career. Over the years I have relied on peers to get through some challenges. In one organization my relationship with a peer on the technology team helped me overcome some significant barriers in a project. Had I not invested the time in cultivating this relationship before we began working together, the project would have likely failed.

Here are a few ways to better understand peers:

- **Conversation**. When you come from outside an organization, your first few weeks should focus on getting to know people and their roles. When you're promoted, you have a new peer group who may be senior to you. You need to get to know them and build relationships. I recommend meeting one-on-one with anyone who is your peer and asking some of these questions.

Before you meet with them, do your homework. Like you would with your direct reports, review their LinkedIn profiles. If you're working in-office, having coffee or lunch is a relaxed way to get to know people. However, a 30-minute virtual call works as well. Here are a few of the questions you might ask your peer:

- ✓ Tell me a little bit about yourself. (Depending on their personality, they will share a little or a lot. Getting to know someone's background will help you connect with them and build a trusting relationship.)
- ✓ What do you enjoy most about working here? (This will help you understand what is important to them and potentially some of their strengths.)
- ✓ How do you think we can best work together? (Skip this if you already know the answer. You could also shift it into a reflection question: "Can you tell me about a time when our areas were working really well together?" Having people reflect on a positive past will create positive emotions.)
- ✓ What advice do you have for me? (Everyone likes to give advice. It's a compliment to the person that you asked. You want to understand if there is anything you should avoid. For example, if something negative happened with the last person in your role, you want to know. Now, be careful not to allow the conversation to turn into gossip. Gossiping may seem like it cements relationships, but in reality, it erodes trust.)

- **Observation.** Notice who goes to lunch together and who they interact with. These signs and symbols create the language of culture you need to understand. Just like in families, there will inevitably be people who don't get along due to feuds and power struggles.

Note: If you are now leading people who were peers before you were promoted, check the website for a specific guide on this situation which will require unique navigation.

Your Boss

We know that the leader-to-teammate relationship is one of the most critical for success. Not liking or respecting who you report to is a recipe for not being your best at work. Hopefully, they're more than your boss—they're your leader.

Here are a few ways to strengthen that connection:

- **Conversation**. Here are some questions to make sure you understand about them:
  - ✓ Tell me your story about how your career has progressed. (How they share their story will be very informative.)
  - ✓ What is your vision for our area/organization?
  - ✓ How do you see our work contributing to the vision?
  - ✓ What are your goals for the year?
  - ✓ How do you prefer to communicate?
- **Observation.** Notice their body language. You understand a lot about interpersonal relationships when you observe how your leader interacts with others. Observe who they talk to and how often others respond to and interact with them.
- **Strengths & Styles.** Work to understand their strengths and personality style. Seek to find ways to complement them (notice the use of an 'e' and not an 'i'). By understanding their strengths, weaknesses, and style, you can find ways to add value.

Your Clients/Customers/Patients/Constituents

An important aspect of understanding your role is staying connected to the customer experience. A friend of ours took over two plants. After hiring, he found out that one was so late on deliveries that their most important customer was ready to leave.

He immediately flew there and shared a turnaround plan. If your clients are internal, get to know them and understand their priorities.

Here are a few ways to increase your understanding:

- **Conversation.** Ask them about themselves. Learn their story to build a foundational relationship. Ask questions like, "What are we doing well? Where can we improve? What can I do to help support your success?"
- **Observation.** Obtain all reports and information that track data related to performance expectations and results for clients. If you have a survey or review data, analyze it in detail. Participate in as many direct customer/client meetings as possible to hear information directly from them.

Other Stakeholders

In many roles, there are other stakeholders you need to know, such as donors, government officials, and other partners. Never underestimate the importance of building relationships before trying to get results. This is the number one reason leaders fail—they go straight to achieving results without understanding the organizational dynamics and relationships.

The next area of the Leaders SUCCEED together© system within understanding is to take a fresh look at your organization as if you were on the outside. If you've recently been hired, maintaining an outside perspective should be easy, and you will likely have insights that are internally unseen. If you're creating a new organization, you have a blank slate to work on, so think about what you would like the organization to be in the future.

3. Organization

Now that you understand your role and stakeholders, you need to understand your organization by taking on the observation skills of a trained consultant. Even if you've been at the organization for twenty years, the way it operates when you take on a new leadership role is unique.

I can't tell you how many clients have told me that their organization appeared one way to them when they were in one job, and then looked totally different from another seat in the company. Just like our view changes depending on where we are sitting in the car, the role we have in the organization requires a different view. General culture usually transcends throughout organizations. However, other pieces, such as the vision/mission/values (VMV), processes, organizational chart, and financials, are worth revisiting.

- **Vision/Mission/Values.** As a leader, you want to add value to the organization. To achieve this, you need to understand where the organization is headed—vision, why they exist—mission, and how people are expected to behave—values. You can usually find these on the website and hear them articulated by key executives. Ensure you also understand any strategies or initiatives from an organizational perspective. Connecting your role and team to key initiatives will increase your impact and value as a leader.
- **Processes.** Processes and procedures are also critical. As someone who honestly hates these types of details (it's often painful for me) but skipping steps or not following norms are other reasons leaders fail. Put on your investigator hat and seek to understand how things are supposed to be done and how they are actually done. Do you have compliance or legal requirements? Are there processes and procedures that could be improved and become easy wins for you as a leader? How can you support others in being more effective and efficient in their roles?

- **Organizational Chart.** Make sure you have a copy of the official organizational chart, so you know who is in the various roles throughout the organization and how your role and department fit into the big picture.
  Just as important is what I call the unpublished organizational chart. It's a complex web of relationships and power that can only be understood if you observe and listen. I've been in organizations where the CEO makes all the decisions. Everyone else is forced to leave their brains at home and do whatever they say. That represents a very clear top-down organizational chart. I've also seen organizations where assistants, project managers, and other seemingly lower-level titles wield more organizational power than the CEO. Using the skills you practiced when you were seeking to understand helps you learn as much as you can about how decisions are made within your organization.
- **Financials.** Even if you work in a non-profit organization, you must pay bills, so revenue inflow is critical to survival. From a leadership perspective, you will immediately be viewed as a more credible leader if you have solid financial acumen and understand how the money is made and spent within the organization. Many leaders are stunted from growing within their organizations because they have avoided understanding finance.
  Regardless of your level as a leader, you need to know how the money is made and spent. Go to the website and download the investor report. If you work for a private organization, spend time with the business analyst or person who handles the budget for the department. Volunteer to be responsible for projects that generate revenue or reduce expenses. These initiatives will give you a unique understanding of the organization that will serve you in the future. As an entrepreneur, cash-flow is king, and one of the main reasons great business ideas fail is because they run

out of money. Planning and caring for finance couldn't be more critical.

As you can see, gaining a much deeper understanding of roles, stakeholders, and the organization is critical for leaders at every level. Whether you've recently been hired from the outside, have been with the company for years, or are running a business on your own, take the time to understand these areas, and you will be more likely to succeed as a leader.

Chapter Summary

This chapter, drawing inspiration from Stephen Covey's famous quote, "Seek first to understand, then to be understood," emphasizes the importance of understanding in leadership. It delves into empathy, its role in becoming the leaders we were meant to be, and how to effectively comprehend and navigate one's role, stakeholders, and the organizational environment.

- **Empathy in Leadership.** Empathy, the ability to understand and share others' feelings, is crucial in leadership. It aids in building trust, enhancing communication, engaging employees, and resolving issues effectively. Leaders are encouraged to learn and practice empathy, even if it doesn't come naturally, as it's more about understanding perspectives than emotional involvement.
- **Three Components of Understanding in the Leaders SUCCEED together© system:**
  1. **Role.** Understanding how your role fits into the organization is vital to your success as a leader and results in more meaningful work.
  2. **Stakeholder.** Identifying and understanding key stakeholders (team, peers, boss, and clients/customers) could mean the difference between success and failure. Engaging

stakeholders involves genuine conversations, active observation, and a curious, non-judgmental approach. Building relationships and trust with stakeholders is also what will make work meaningful.

3. **Organization.** Successful leaders have a broader organizational mindset. They understand context, including mission, vision, values, processes, the organizational chart, and financials. Understanding these elements helps align leadership actions with the organization's direction and culture.

- **Practical Approaches.** Using the conversation guides and other practical methods to understand your role, stakeholders, and the organization will help you develop a new understanding of how you can succeed.
  Leaders who invest time and effort to deeply understand their roles, stakeholders, and organizational dynamics are difference makers. This understanding, grounded in empathy, enables you to navigate complex environments, build strong relationships, and make informed decisions.

Now, let's Do, Reflect, and Discuss, which helps us gain a deeper understanding as we work toward becoming the leaders we were meant to be.

Do

1. Locate your job description and goals for your position. If you are an entrepreneur or don't have a job description or goals, write down 3-5 goals for this month and for this year. What do you really want to accomplish?
2. Review the conversation starters in the chapter and use those questions with some key stakeholders.

3. Find or establish your organization's vision, mission, and values.

Reflect

1. What are the journeys of your team, boss, and key stakeholders? How can you improve your connections based on these new understandings?
2. Which stakeholders have you been overlooking? Are there other people you need to talk with? Is there a relationship you need to improve?
3. How do your personal values align with the organization? Are there places you are misaligned, and how can you get these more in sync?

Discuss

1. Share a time you were in a role with unclear goals or a mismatch between the job description and what you were doing. Explain how you establish job descriptions and goals within your organization, and how you leverage your strengths.
2. Provide information about your key stakeholders and the relationships that are positive or could be improved.
3. Download the empathy exercise on the website and practice it with the group.

Chapter 4: Communication

The Leadership Bridge

As I mentioned earlier, I struggled with academics. However, during college I learned that I could communicate. Communication became my superpower. It built my confidence, and I began taking on leadership roles on campus.

I enjoyed working with other people. Sharing information was my pathway to earning A's. After college, my manager was amazed by my ability to analyze data and present information in a way that was accessible to everyone. I continued leveraging this strength throughout my career.

As I was promoted from roles within operations to sales, I learned new communication skills. I understood how to rally team members around a shared vision, building a successful sales team across seven sites led by talented VPs who worked with me to achieve significant year-over-year double digit growth. I loved leading teams, building new departments, and achieving success together.

Seemingly, I had a achieved my dreams when I become a senior vice-president of a global bank and won their national leadership award three years in a row. I should have been satisfied, right? Oh, if only I had made my life so simple. Instead, I began to think to myself, *well, I've excelled at sales and operations, maybe I should try my hand at marketing. It was my other college major.*

But the only marketing roles open internally were in New York, and I couldn't relocate my family. Searching around on my laptop one evening, I replied to a LinkedIn ad for a senior marketing director position. I got the job and left people and a career I had enjoyed for almost ten years.

After a week buried in product manuals, I knew I had made a big mistake. I didn't like being a sole contributor. It sounded good at first—not having leadership responsibility—but I missed leading people. I also found that I couldn't measure my success as easily as I could in operations and sales.

I tried to make the role work, but the harder I tried, the more miserable I became. My performance suffered—along with my health. I ended up in the hospital three times. Once for a bleeding ulcer and twice for chest pain.

At the yearly sales event, it all came crashing down. My leader had asked me to give a presentation, and I didn't even take time to prepare. I assumed I could present on autopilot. I thought, *I do this all the time. I don't need to prepare.*

I barely flipped through my slides the night before and got up in front of the room and began my talk. Suddenly, the room felt like it was spinning. I was sweating like I'd just gotten out of a sauna, and I couldn't remember anything I was supposed to talk about.

I saw the horrified look on my leader's face and thought, *Oh no, I am blowing this. And she trusted me.* I quickly flipped through the slides and then sat down. Everyone was staring at me like, "What just happened?"

At the next break my leader said, "Hey, what was that about?"

Embarrassed and unsure, I said, "I guess I don't feel well. I didn't eat breakfast." But I knew it was more than physical. I had failed to prepare. I had been so focused on myself and why I didn't like my job that I let the team down by not representing our department well.

Unfortunately, after that presentation I started having panic attacks any time I had to present. It got so bad that I had difficulty even speaking in meetings. These would continue for years—even after I left that job. I had lost my superpower. I had taken for granted the gift of communication, and I was having to relearn it from the start.

This relearning process, however, set me on a journey of discovery. I researched the best communicators and communication strategies—the findings of which I will share will you here. It also gave me a deep empathy for people who fear public speaking more than death, as many do.

Through my research I also learned that the greatest communicators practice, sometimes for months, when they are working on sharing important messages. Steve Jobs, the founder of Apple, rehearsed for hours before the talks he gave, all of which appeared natural and unscripted.[20]

Presentations are a unique challenge for many of us, but what about day-to-day communication? We all communicate.

Have you ever received an email and thought, *What is this person talking about?* Or attended a meeting and wondered why your valuable time was being wasted?

Conversely, have you ever been so moved by a leader talking about their vision that you couldn't help but feel the pull and desire to do whatever was necessary to be part of it? Have you seen the smile on a coworker's face when they were acknowledged for doing a great job? Or maybe you felt this sense of accomplishment for yourself when you received recognition? This is all communication. It's the bridge we use to connect to people.

Why Communication?

Communication is one of the most important aspects of leadership. It separates great leaders from those who are mediocre. For leaders, communication is critical to success.

In all communication, you have a sender and a receiver. It may be one-to-one or one-to-many. It isn't easy because we all have a filter through which we receive and process information.

Despite our best efforts to relay the message as received, some changes are always made to the original message. It can be attributed to our state of mind or how we perceive it from the speaker. Leaders who communicate in an easily understood language (even vernacular) leave no room for ambiguity.

I've worked in places that provided a dictionary of commonly used terms to new hires. Acronyms and phrases run rampant in banking, healthcare and higher education. I'll never forget when my boss asked me to bring a deck to the meeting. I had no idea what she was saying and was too embarrassed to ask.

Fortunately, I asked a peer before heading to the hardware store. Now that I do a lot of coaching in healthcare, I remind myself that CMO stands for Chief Medical Officer in hospitals and Chief Marketing Officer in other organizations. Having empathy for people in new roles and kindly explaining terms you may take for granted will improve communication.

Leaders communicate verbally and non-verbally—in writing and in how they respond to conflicts and coach others, which all come together to influence culture and engagement (covered in later chapters).

For now, let's focus on how we can use the Leaders SUCCEED together© system by 1. Leveraging the 8 Cs of effective communication, 2. Embracing conflict, and 3. Integrating coaching with our leadership style to maximize effectiveness.

1. 8 Cs

There are 8 Cs of communication that I have found to be an easy-to-use checklist for leaders to follow. The next time you prepare to communicate, check for the 8 Cs.

1. **Care.** "Nobody cares how much you know until they know how much you care." This quote is often attributed to Theodor Roosevelt, but no known author exists. However, it's first on the list because it sets the stage for how the rest of your message will be received. How are you communicating that you care about the other person or audience?
2. **Clarity.** The information shared should be well-organized, clear, cohesive, and concise. Rambling emails and conversations with no structure leave team members confused and unsure of what to do. Come to meetings with an agenda, be specific if you're asking for information and eliminate unnecessary words that could lead to confusion. Ask yourself: Am I being clear in my communication? Are there ways I can be more concise, so my core message isn't being lost?
3. **Connection.** "Connecting is the ability to identify with people and relate to them in a way that increases your influence." (John C. Maxwell). Humans are social animals. As a species, we look to make connections and thrive on them. Communication is the

most essential form of human connection. It allows us to understand one another and be understood. The level of connection between people is directly proportional to effective communication. We also want to understand how concepts are related, so if you share a new initiative, connect it to the organizational mission and other initiatives you have going on now. How are you connecting to the audience or other people? How is what you're communicating connected to other concepts people are familiar with or the organizational mission?

4. **Confidence.** Word choice, tone of voice, use of technology, and non-verbal communication should exude confidence without arrogance, building your credibility as a leader. We want to follow people who are confident in themselves and in what they are saying. Using a language that is not easily understood, a condescending tone, or not being proficient in using technology reduces your credibility. How are you demonstrating confidence in your communication?
5. **Competence.** Stephen Covey cites competence and character as two core components of trust, which we know is at the center of leadership. A few ways to demonstrate competence-yet-humility are: Leading by example, clearly articulating your thoughts, listening actively, focusing on solving problems, and not blaming people. Instead, empower people and commit to continuous learning.
6. **Consistency.** One area I hear people complain about is how leaders are inconsistent in their communication. Remember, self-leadership is important, so if you're having a bad day and can't get a handle on your emotions, it's probably best to wait to communicate an important message. We want leaders we follow to be consistent in how and what they communicate because it creates a culture of stability and confidence. How are you demonstrating consistency in your communication?

7. **Character.** Trust is the foundation of leadership and communicating with character builds trust. This means speaking honestly, avoiding gossip, never talking poorly about people, and keeping the confidence of others. How are you demonstrating character in your communication? How do people know they can trust you?
8. **Call to Action.** An often-missed opportunity for leaders is to use a familiar advertising and marketing strategy for communication—a call to action. Remember, if leadership is influence, if you're working to influence your audience to follow you, you likely want them to do something. Being clear about what you need people to do and how they can be part of something bigger than themselves will improve the effectiveness of your communication. What are you asking people to do? Is it clear how they can be part of what you're sharing?

Watch Out for Derailers

Watch out for two things: Humble bragging and letting your ego get the best of you. I've been guilty of both, so I'm talking to myself as well. Often, people will try to appear humble by making falsely self-deprecating statements. For example, "I'm not very smart, so I barely squeaked by at Harvard." Or, outright self-deprecation: "With my looks, I should be on the radio." When you use these methods of communication, you make your audience uncomfortable. I've also heard people brag about humility, saying things like, "I'm too humble to boast, but . . ." Or you'll see a LinkedIn professionals post, "I'm humbled to win this award."

Although we all want accolades for our achievements, when it comes across as bragging-disguised-as-humility, you won't connect with your audience, and trust-building may be at risk. Be natural and follow the 8 Cs to increase your impact through communicating as a leader.

Now, let's talk about conflict, another potential derailer for leadership communication.

2. Conflict

Outside of self-awareness, conflict-avoidance is the second biggest career derailer I see in my consulting and coaching practice. Conflict-avoidance is so common it's like I'm helping someone resolve a conflict every day. Whether or not we want to admit it, most of us hate conflict.

For many of us, the idea of conflict is akin to having major surgery. But I assure you, if you rewire your brain to see conflict as simple communication and not a battle to be fought, you will increase your influence as a leader.

Leadership is about relationships, so there are bound to be conflicts that require communication. As I've said, conflict is one of the most frequent issues for leaders I work with, and it almost became a chapter of its own. But I decided not to give conflict that much power.

Although most people are conflict-avoidant, some personalities go at it head-on. I have a friend who is never afraid of conflict. She is an Enneagram 8. One of the core traits of that personality type is that they never back away from a good argument. My friend has shared that she feels the need to address issues. Otherwise, she fears they will become bigger and take on a life of their own. She also doesn't understand why some people like to avoid conflict.

For those who are highly conflict-avoidant, someone addressing issues could be misinterpreted as arguing, leaving them feeling like they've been hit by a bus. The personality differences discussed in the self-awareness chapter can be applied to a person's conflict tolerance. These wirings are important to understand about ourselves and those we work with daily.

Conflict is an inevitable part of any workplace. Successful leaders find ways to resolve conflict and use it as an opportunity to deepen relationships and improve workplace culture. But how?

Here is a five-step strategy for leaders to manage and embrace conflict:

1. **Address the conflicts promptly.** Someone in one of my leadership sessions approached me. "I need your help," he said. "A person on my team was late 71 times this year." I asked when he first noticed she was late. He said, "The first time. But I was afraid to address it." I explained that by avoiding conflict, he set the standard that coming to work at a specific time was not required. He had reinforced the behavior as acceptable.
   Alternatively, if he had commented on her tardiness the first time, he would have likely avoided the entire situation. He could have said, "Is everything alright? I noticed you were late today." But he didn't. As you can see, when we don't address conflict, problems are rarely resolved. The faster we address it, the better. Delaying action can cause a conflict to become more entrenched and difficult to resolve. My only caveat is that you shouldn't address conflict if you're angry or upset. It's best to wait a day or so and then have a rational conversation.
2. **Establish standards of professionalism.** Leaders are responsible for making clear what is and is not acceptable. Based on the culture and goals of the organization, leaders set the tone for what is and is not acceptable. Not only in how we treat one another, but also that certain standards of professionalism are expected in the workplace. Be clear about these—respecting every person, not interrupting one another, not sharing information that isn't ours to share, not raising our voices, etc. When team members see conflict managed professionally, it

provides an example for everyone to follow. If, however, leaders allow people to raise their voices, hurl insults, and handle conflict inappropriately in the workplace, it will eventually become the norm and damage the culture.

3. **Listen actively.** Listening actively and empathetically can build trust with those involved in the conflict. It can also help you better understand everyone's issues and perspectives. So often we are thinking about what we'll say next to prove our point in an argument that we don't even hear what the person said. In managing conflict, listening is one of the most important skills to cultivate. You observe and learn what's really going on with the other person and can flex your style to connect with them versus pushing them away.
4. **Identify common ground.** Look for areas of agreement and shared goals between the parties involved. Focusing on common ground can help to build consensus and move towards resolution. Common ground doesn't mean compromise, where both people have to lose something. It can mean a win-win or win-lose as well. It's just about finding a solution that supports the overall goals of the organization and maintains dignity for each individual.
5. **Collaborate on a solution.** If possible, develop a mutually acceptable solution to the conflict that each person has a part in crafting. As a leader, if you jump in and resolve every issue your team members have with one another, you're creating a hierarchical leadership structure and giving everyone else permission to mentally check out. If, however, you require that those involved in conflict actively participate in resolving their issues with one another, you're teaching those you work with a skill they can use in every aspect of their life. Recently, someone told me that their daughter, who just graduated college, brought an issue with a coworker to her boss. He guided her in resolving

the conflict on her own without letting the other person know she had involved him. Wow, now that is leadership! We are called to empower people to resolve conflicts on their own and become the leaders they were meant to be.

Remember, reframing conflict in your mind as just having a conversation takes much of the fear out of it. I have had countless coaching sessions where clients have made elaborate predictions about how a potential conflict conversation would unfold, and very rarely has their theory become reality. Not addressing the conflict sooner is the one regret most leaders I coach have had. Because once the conflict has been resolved, it feels like a giant weight is lifted off their shoulders. So, don't wait! Have that conversation you've been putting off today.

3. Coaching

One evening I sat by a fire and listened to my friend's daughter tell a story about her first job out of college. She spent almost an hour sharing how her boss had monthly one-on-one coaching sessions with her as required. Unfortunately, her boss spent that hour telling her that she wasn't doing a good job (providing no specific examples) and said that, by the way, no one liked her. The only positive experience she remembered was her manager's surprise and dismay on the day she resigned. Only then did her manager's story change. "We're sorry and disappointed to see you leave."

How could there be such a disconnect?

I explained to the young woman that we can learn so much about becoming a better leader from negative experiences. Bad bosses teach us a lot about how *not* to lead and how it feels when someone does not live up to their leadership potential. On the inside I was furious that one manager could negatively impact a young person.

No wonder we have retention problems in so many organizations—there's little focus on developing these frontline leaders. This is why the third core component of communication is coaching.

Here is a proven strategy for coaching communication that works well:

- **Near-Immediate.** A leader in one of my leadership development sessions shared with me that he had an employee who had not made their goals for five months, and they were ready to fire him. I asked how many coaching conversations they had so far, and he said he hadn't talked with the person because he was waiting for their six-month review. I asked how his team member might know he wasn't meeting expectations, and he said everyone could see the reports. I then asked if he knew why the team member wasn't meeting goals and what they might need to be successful. He just stared at me with a curious expression. He hadn't considered discussing performance outside of a formal review process. Unfortunately, this happens often with new supervisors because they are so focused on doing what they need to succeed in their role that they forget to bring those around them along. Fortunately, he committed to near-immediate coaching. This is why I am so passionate about bringing these leadership lessons to frontline supervisors. They are critical to the organization's success and often overlooked. I take it further than many people who say timely coaching is important. I use the term *near-immediate,* because the closer the time is between the situation and the coaching, the more likely the person is to remember. Especially if it is positive and something you want them to continue doing, then you have to recognize them immediately.
  Think about it: If I wait for two weeks to talk to you about behavior, how likely is it that you will remember what you did? I can barely remember what I ate for breakfast this morning. The sooner we talk to someone, the more likely they will be to recall

the specifics in order to repeat or change their behavior. Let's explore the characteristics of near-immediate coaching.

- **Individualized.** Everyone likes to receive coaching a little differently. Even if you have a standardized process of weekly one-on-ones, you can provide near-immediate feedback outside of that structure—in the way someone will receive it best. I had a manager who cried every time I gave her negative feedback in person. But I noticed that I could call her on the phone and have a good conversation where she didn't break down. To honor her dignity, I called her when providing positive and negative feedback, and I set up our coaching sessions in person to discuss goal setting and progress. Personally, with my facial expressions I find difficult to control, I would much rather receive negative feedback over the phone to better manage how I process the information. From a positive feedback perspective, a friend told me how uncomfortable it made her when her boss constantly praised her in front of others in the office because the comments made her a target of jealousy and backstabbing from her coworkers. She asked him to please praise her in private, and they had a great conversation about how she is best rewarded.
- **Aligned with Our Culture.** Another leader I know berated employees on conference calls and was then perplexed as to why no one ever admitted to making mistakes and why employees constantly blamed one another. How we coach our team members through feedback impacts people *and* culture. Hence, we need to know people as individuals to discover their preferences—to understand how the feedback we're sharing could impact our culture. We also need to connect how we provide coaching with our core values and make sure we're upholding these.
- **Specific.** The goal of communicating feedback through coaching is to help someone continue or discontinue behaviors and

improve overall. If we aren't specific when communicating, the team members won't know how to improve. For example, instead of saying that the presentation was sloppy, we need to say that on pages 10 and 12 there were numerical errors, and on page 22, the graphic was blurry. How much easier is fixing something when we know exactly what is wrong? Conversely, saying, "Great job," without sharing what was great about it also doesn't help us grow. Instead, say, "Great job explaining the purpose of the project and engaging the team in dialogue." Or, "I appreciate how you're connecting so well with our customers, given the emails I've been receiving about the support you are providing."

- **Dialogue.** One of my favorite questions when coaching is, "How do you think that went?" It allows the person to share their perspective. Eight out of ten times, they identified the gaps that I was going to share. It's much more effective for us to self-diagnose where we need to improve versus having someone tell us what we need to do. Asking questions sets the stage for dialogue. Also, refrain from using language that ignites a firestorm of emotion. For example, "Why did you do this? What were you thinking? How could you let this happen?" These phrases trigger an immediate protective response that limits dialogue and rarely produces positive outcomes.
- **Solution-Focused.** Have you ever heard the phrase, "It's not personal. It's just business."? Wrong. What we do as leaders always impacts people personally. You can't separate your personal and professional self. It's why we need to remain solution-focused when it comes to coaching. I like to use a coaching method called TGROW—Topic, Goal, Reality, Options, and Way Forward. It is a great conversation framework that always ends with a way forward. You have the person suggest a solution and then agree on it together through dialogue before closing the conversation. During this process,

you focus on growth and development; even more importantly, the person should know you care.

Conflict & Coaching Watchouts

There are two areas to watch with conflict and coaching. One is timing, and the other is this concept called radical candor or transparency.

1. **Timing.** There are three exceptions I find appropriate to delay coaching or difficult conversations. First, when it's obvious that the person or people involved are emotional about the situation, I will wait a day or two until things settle down. Second, when I'm frustrated and do not believe I can self-manage enough to discuss appropriately. Third, when I need counsel from HR, legal, my leader, or even a coach on how to handle the situation best. Timeliness is still important because leadership is about relationships, and think about what would happen if your spouse or best friend came to you with a list of infractions they had been tracking? Can you imagine if they took out their phone and began reading a list, saying, "On June 10th, you said this, and it was disrespectful to me. On July 4th, you did that, and that was rude." It would be hard to trust that person because you would always be walking on eggshells, worried that they were watching everything you did to add things to their list. I have heard some divorced couples say that their ex behaved this way, and it left them on edge and eventually eroded the marriage. One evening I was in Walmart and a woman came up and hugged me, saying that my virtual course about conflict saved her marriage because she didn't realize this is what she was doing with her husband. I had never met her in-person but hugged her back because I was so happy for her.

2. **Radical Candor or Transparency.** I have had clients tell me that they were just being 'radically candid' or 'transparent' when they told a person what they thought without any regard to their feelings. I believe this concept is being misappropriated. When people say whatever they want—regardless of how hurtful and rude it comes across—they can't just label it as being transparent, candid, or direct as an excuse. The reality is that it damages relationships and can have a serious impact on the culture. So even if honesty is part of your core values, as it is mine, we still must share information in a way that maintains dignity. Establishing guidelines for how you treat one another and ensuring they are followed protects your culture from these pitfalls.

Remember, communication is critical to leadership. As leaders, we are responsible for communicating effectively by leveraging the 8 Cs, managing conflict, and coaching our teams to become the best versions of themselves. Great leaders are great communicators who inspire the people around them, making everyone feel heard and valued. Try just a few of the ideas in this chapter and see how much more connection and trust you will build.

Chapter Summary

The role of communication in leadership is like a bridge that connects leaders to people. Effective communication can inspire, engage, and influence in both personal and professional settings.

- **Importance of Communication in Leadership.** When you take learning to communicate more effectively as an ongoing journey of improving daily, you will see build better relationships and organizational culture.

- **Three Components of Communication in the Leaders SUCCEED together© system:**
  1. **The 8 Cs of Effective Communication.**
     1) Care: Showing genuine concern for others.
     2) Clarity: Ensuring messages are clear, concise, and well-structured.
     3) Connection: Relating to others to increase influence and understanding.
     4) Confidence: Communicating assertively without arrogance.
     5) Competence: Demonstrating knowledge and skill as a leader through communication.
     6) Consistency: Maintaining a stable and predictable communication style.
     7) Character: Building trust through honesty and integrity.
     8) Call to Action: Clearly articulating desired actions or responses.
  2. **Managing Conflict.** Embrace conflict as a natural aspect of relationships by addressing conflicts promptly and professionally, using active listening and identifying common ground.
  3. **Integrating Coaching in Communication.** By coaching effectively, encouraging dialogue, and supporting team members, leaders demonstrate they care about the success of everyone.
- **Avoiding Communication Pitfalls**. Be wary of 'humblebragging' and ego-driven communication. Also, watch out for radical candor and extreme transparency that can damage relationships.

Effective communication is vital for leaders, encompassing empathy, clarity, and the ability to resolve conflicts and coach others. By mastering the 8 Cs of communication, embracing conflict, and investing in coaching, leaders can enhance their influence, build trust, and foster a positive workplace culture. Leaders who refine their communication skills convey their messages effectively and respond to others empathetically. They set the stage for successful leadership and healthy organizational dynamics.

Now, let's take time to improve our communication skills within the Leaders SUCCEED together© system by Doing, Reflecting, and Discussing the insights we have gained in this chapter.

Do

1. Locate an email, letter, or presentation where you communicated recently and evaluate it against the 8 Cs. See where you did well and where you can improve. Record a meeting and measure yourself against the 8 Cs.
2. Identify a situation where there is conflict and address it using the model described in the chapter.
3. Practice the TGROW coaching model described with a team member.

Reflect

1. Which of the 8 Cs are your strengths, and where could you improve?
2. How did a recent conflict situation go? What went well, and where might you improve?
3. What is going well with how you are coaching, and where might you improve?

Discuss

1. Discuss leaders who are great communicators and which of the 8Cs they do well. Which ones are your strengths?
2. Discuss how you typically deal with conflict and what would happen if you began to view conflict as conversation.
3. Share a time when you felt successful at coaching someone.

Chapter 5: Culture

The Leadership Soil

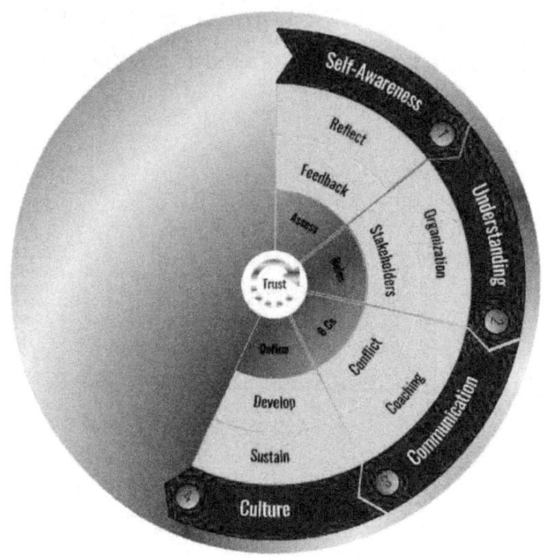

Culture within organizations is fascinating to me. As a consultant, you can see the differences easily in signs, symbols, and language between one workplace to the next. It shows up at the first meeting.

Several years ago, a leader from a private company contacted me and said she was referred to me by someone because everyone knows that I build departments and am really good at customer and employee engagement. Flattered, of course, I was happy to accept the meeting and find out what they needed. They were consolidating their customer service across the country and had project managers but needed a strategist who could look at the entire system and help them build it.

I arrived onsite and in the parking lot were front-row executive parking spaces where brand new F-150s were parked. The building was old but in good condition and the cars in front were new. The two women who greeted me in the lobby were friendly and warm. We sat in a conference room and talked about the project, and it sounded interesting to me.

Then they looked at each other and their watches and said, "OK, we should go upstairs to meet one of the owners. We said we would be there at two, and it's one forty-five."

I sensed urgency in their voices, so I assumed we had a long way to travel. I jumped up and said, "Let's go."

We headed to the top floor of the building and stood outside a giant mahogany door with an intercom. They pressed the button and announced our arrival, and we went inside. The furnishings were antique, and everything had its place. The women left me sitting on the lobby couch and said they would be back.

At exactly 2:00 PM a receptionist took me to the office of one of the owners. A big man in his fifties walked out behind one of the largest desks I have ever seen and shook my hand. He began by asking me about my family.

He asked what my parents did. I told him my mom was a nurse and my dad, a machinist. We talked about where I grew up before discussing my experience and how I could help them.

At the end of the meeting, he stood up and said, "We're going to hire you because I think you come from good stock."

I was excited about the opportunity and called my mom on the way home. When I told her I got the new client because I was from good stock, she was happy I got the job but wasn't sure about being compared to cattle.

What I learned during that one interview would serve me well throughout the three years of consulting work I did for them. Most of the people had been farmers, and they prided themselves on working hard. If you weren't fifteen minutes early to a meeting, you were late. They had almost no attrition despite their hierarchical leadership style. They cared deeply about their people and their families.

What Is Culture?

Culture refers to shared beliefs, values, attitudes, behaviors, and practices that characterize a particular group or organization. It encompasses the norms, traditions, and customs shaping how individuals interact and function within a social or work environment.[21] It's a "complex set of values, beliefs, assumptions, and symbols that define how a firm does business."[22]

For me, culture is the personality of an organization. People create a culture under the supervision of their leaders and continue to add to it over time. Cultures evolve as organizations change. We, as leaders, are responsible for continuously designing a culture that leads to growth for people and the organization.

Sometimes leaders say, "We have a serious culture problem at my workplace." My response is to seek to understand what they mean and, at some point, reinforce that, as leaders, we own culture because our actions are part of what creates culture.

Sure, sometimes we are dealt toxic cultures when we move into an organization and are asked to fix it. However, more often, culture problems gradually develop, like mold growing on a basement wall. They take over slowly, remaining under the surface before bursting out and damaging the entire organization.

Leaders navigate many cultural challenges in organizations as people from diverse cultures often come together to form the organizational culture. Just like people, every organization has a unique personality. And, just like soil quality impacts plants, fruits, and vegetables, workplace culture is the difference between a healthy work environment and a toxic one.

Cultural Differences

As I sit here and type this chapter from Lyon, France, I'm reminded of the impact of culture everywhere I look. My husband had a meeting here and asked me to come along. I thought the trip might allow me to concentrate on this book while he was working, and fortunately, much of my consulting can be done virtually. I jumped at the offer.

His team is here for a global sales meeting to bring the leaders across countries together to align strategies. Organizations benefit significantly from getting everyone in the same room to collaborate, and it's great to see leaders investing in holding monthly or quarterly onsite meetings to develop themselves, work together, and create connections.

I have traveled to various countries for work throughout my career. Being in a place where I don't speak the language reinforces the concept of culture. It prompts me to think about how we can create culture within our organizations. Everything you do feels normal if it's part of a particular culture you understand.

Culture is everywhere. The soil where I live in Kentucky is brown, but I typically ignore it until I travel west and see the bright red canyons. It's only then that I note the difference. I'm sure you've noticed cultural differences if you've ever traveled to another country or, sometimes, another state.

If you work in a multinational company, you will want to be aware of cultural differences for each location you are responsible for. For instance, a leader who had recently taken over a global sales team shared that whenever he had meetings, he wasn't getting a lot of participation from his sales leaders in Asia. However, his North American sales team was constantly sharing ideas.

I asked if he sent the agenda beforehand, letting them know the meeting's topics. I asked if he was specifically requesting the 'quiet' attendees for their thoughts versus leaving the floor open for whoever wanted to speak.

He said he wasn't doing either. I shared some insight and recommended a book about cultural intelligence by David Livermore. He shifted his approach based on the generally accepted norms of the cultures he was leading and found much more success. Unfortunately, I had to learn this the hard way years before I began executive coaching.

I was traveling in the Philippines on a consulting assignment to implement a sales and marketing strategy I had successfully applied throughout the United States. My guide in Manila was a project manager named Leah who had worked with the site locations for many years.

During our first stop at one of the contact centers, I delivered my typical high-energy presentation, sharing the plan that had worked in the US. The leaders seemed to be satisfied with the idea, smiling and nodding their heads. Their English was impeccable, which was evident from their verbalized positive remarks. As we left the building, I patted myself on the back for another successful implementation of the sales and marketing strategy.

However, my gut feeling was that something was wrong. Though I couldn't put my finger on it, I knew a puzzle piece was missing. I slumped in my seat as we sat in the car. I looked at Leah and said, "They didn't agree with anything I said, did they?"

She looked straight ahead and said, "Nope."

It was a humble moment, and yet, a wonderful opportunity for learning. I asked, "What did I do wrong?"

She explained a few things I should have known but hadn't considered. First, being a senior director from the US headquarters meant they would not disagree with me openly. Secondly, my high-energy, excited approach was a turn-off to this group, as they expected an executive with a more measured communication style. I had also not shared anything in advance. I basically showed up on their doorstep with the plan and *then* asked for their thoughts about it.

Wow, I thought. *I was acting like a jerk.*

These failures, or missteps as we might categorize them, are exceptional learning opportunities. Over lunch, I sat with Leah and, with her guidance, revamped my approach. We found that by beginning with an open discussion, and caring for some specific nuances, the approach would work better in this country. We were able to adjust and ultimately have a successful rollout.

Culture Preferences

As I've said, culture is like personality. Everyone you meet won't be your best friend, and not every workplace culture is right for everyone. There are many organizational cultures, but some are better than others for people, depending on their personality. That's why we start with self-awareness in the Leaders SUCCEED together© system.

One person may believe the company culture is terrific, while another may find it toxic. You can see these conflicting reviews on Glassdoor, where one employee may rate the company high, and another, low.

However, there are some cultures where no one can deny the problems. Research has also found that a firm's culture can create higher financial performance and be a source of a sustainable competitive advantage if it is rare, valuable, and imperfectly imitable.[23]

Suppose you can intentionally create and maintain a positive and unique culture. In that case, it has the potential to create immense value for your customers and employees and may be difficult (if not impossible) for competitors to mimic.

Within the Leaders SUCCEED together© system, we can succeed by being intentional in how we 1. Define, 2. Develop, and 3. Sustain positive work cultures.

1. Define

The first step in intentionally designing culture is to define the current culture. If you're an entrepreneur just starting out, you get to define your culture and build it. If you're a solopreneur working on your own, you can use this section to think about the cultures of the clients you would like to serve.

One of the things I love about my consulting practice is that I get to choose which client cultures I work with. For instance, there have been times when I have passed on business when I believe that a client doesn't care about their employees or is unwilling to change. There are many organizational cultures, yet none is right for everyone.

Sometimes I hear people describe cultures, and when I begin to work with the client, I realize things are not as they seem. Here are some ways to define your current culture and understand if it's working for you.

- **Employee Surveys.** Conduct anonymous surveys to gather feedback from employees. I have conducted these surveys for organizations across industries, and they can be very insightful—especially if you take the time to read and understand the comments.
- **Cautions for Surveys**
  - **How They Are Conducted.** Almost every organization will say that they conduct employee engagement or culture surveys. However, how these are administered and reported

also speaks of the culture. For instance, there is a company I know well where employees often complain about the workplace culture. Even Glassdoor ratings and reviews are consistently poor. Employees from the past and present have shared stories with me about the abusive and threatening culture. Even with the well-known reputation of having a toxic culture, the company has won awards for being the "best place to work." It even touts this on its website and advertising. Since I'm always curious, I often ask people to share their experience of the employee survey process at their work, and you would be surprised by how many people at this company shared comments like these:

- "These surveys are a joke. No one reads any of the results, and they act like they care about what we think."
- "The reason our employee engagement is so high is because my manager threatened us that if we didn't give good scores, they would find out who said what and fire people."
- "I told my employees that if they didn't respond positively to the employee survey, then we would all be in trouble and have to answer to corporate and work on action plans for months."
- "Are they seriously thinking that any of us will provide sincere feedback when HR collects the data? I'm not stupid. They have my IP address and there is no way this is anonymous."
- "My boss told us that he would buy a round of drinks for all of us if we won the award for best places to work. Who doesn't want free drinks?"

o **Bias.** As with any research, there can be bias in various ways. You will also have employees who deliberately answer negatively because they have an axe to grind against their boss or coworkers, further affecting the results. My biggest advice regarding using employee surveys to assess culture is to look at this information as one data point in conjunction with other quantitative and qualitative data.

- **Incentives.** I also never advise clients to use employee engagement or satisfaction as part of informal or formal incentive programs. Some will argue that what gets incentivized gets done, but the potential for biased data-gathering is too significant in these internal surveys.
- **Survey Administration.** I also recommend that a third party conduct the surveys, and not because I do this in my consulting practice. Remember, I care deeply about your success, so you can use anyone you choose, but please avoid sending employee satisfaction surveys internally for two reasons. One reason is based on some of the comments I mentioned earlier—the assumption that the surveys aren't truly anonymous. For two, I've been part of situations within organizations where certain department leaders didn't receive the results they hoped for. Since HR gathered the data, they were the ones who took the heat, building animosity between HR and that department. Either situation is unfavorable for organizational cultures, so it's best to avoid surveying internally if possible.
- **Observational Analysis.** Just like anthropologists and social science researchers have used for centuries, observation can be a powerful tool to assess culture. There used to be a phrase you would hear called management by walking around. This means the best managers leave their offices to observe and interact with people. As I mentioned at the beginning of this chapter, when we travel to another country and experience different cultures, it's easy to notice our environment. I could

read books and articles about France, but visiting and interacting with France's people will allow me to understand the culture more deeply. To succeed at assessing culture, leaders take time to observe daily interactions, team dynamics, and overall employee behavior. Pay particular attention to signs of stress, conflict, disengagement, and moments of collaboration and positivity. I often work with clients to assess culture and observe meetings and interactions for cues. As an outsider, it's easier for me to pick up on what is unique about the culture and what the areas for improvement might be.

For example, I went into a bathroom once at a client location and saw a big sign that said, "Do NOT put anything in the toilets. -Management." In contrast, another client had a sign in the bathroom that said, "Please help us avoid plumbing problems by not placing anything in the toilet." These are simple signs that demonstrate differences in cultures. Once I gather the data through observations, I check back with the client to determine whether what I observed matches or conflicts with the culture they believe to be in place. This exercise provides insight, giving a clearer view of the organization's culture.

- **Focus Groups/Personal Interviews.** Another opportunity to assess culture is by conducting carefully designed focus groups or interviews. This qualitative data gathering can be very effective. In focus groups, a facilitator asks various pre-determined questions and gathers qualitative data to understand the norms of the organization and how it functions.

  Similarly, personal interviews are designed with open-ended, standard questions asked one-on-one in a confidential setting with employees of various levels of the organization. I prefer the one-on-one interviews due to the depth of the data untainted by other opinions, but both can be used together in a cultural assessment. Again, another note of caution about using internal resources: Even in situations with an open and transparent culture, don't expect to get unbiased data by using internal resources to collect it. The risk is too high for most employees to tell you something you don't want to hear.

- **Review Policies and Procedures.** In one consulting engagement, my objective was to improve the customer experience. When asked to work on this in an organization, I always include the employee experience, because the culture we create for employees directly impacts the customer. This action of assessing culture requires leaders to evaluate existing policies, procedures, and management practices to identify any contributing to a positive or negative work culture. Here is where leaders should look for discrepancies between stated values and actual practices.

  For instance, I once attended a seminar where the CEO talked about a core value: simplicity. He cited examples of how they focus on making things simple for customers. However, having consulted with the organization, I knew that their complex policies and procedures made work as difficult as possible for employees and impacted their culture. With such a disconnect between espoused values for the customer experience and what employees experience, the culture can become negative. Another example is when employees see values posted on the wall that are not actually prioritized.

  For example, one company I've worked with had integrity as a core value. Yet, employees shared that unethical issues were not being addressed, leaving them to roll their eyes every day they walked under the values statements posted above the door. In the next section of this chapter, we will see that intentionally creating culture rests on living out stated values. Therefore, matching processes, procedures, and the lived reality of employees with the stated organizational values is core to assessing culture.

Once leaders have defined the current work culture, if there are areas to improve the culture for their team or department, the next step within the Leaders SUCCEED together© system is to develop a more positive work culture.

2. Develop

Whenever I hear people say that they don't like the culture at work, I find that sometimes it's a toxic culture or a bad fit for that person. However, at other times, I find that those who are complaining the loudest contribute to what they dislike most about the culture. Everyone can impact the culture at work, and we all need to take responsibility for how we influence our work culture.

Culture as a Competitive Advantage

We know that the workplace is not merely a space for completing tasks—it's a dynamic ecosystem where people spend a significant portion of their lives. Therefore, developing a positive work culture is how leaders succeed in creating places where team members get excited every day to come to work.

We want teams who are energized and leveraging their strengths. Not only is intentionally developing culture good for people, but it can also be a strategic advantage for the organization because culture is almost impossible for competitors to replicate.

Think about it. Competitors can copy your products, services, or technology. But they cannot copy your culture, so this is where you can jump ahead and develop a core competitive advantage.

Here are some specific focus areas for you in developing a positive culture:

- **Define Core Values.** As I mentioned in the chapter on communication, defining core values is critical for effective leadership, as these values lay the foundation for work culture. Determining and articulating the organization's core values and beliefs differentiates acceptable and unacceptable behavior. This process distinguishes your culture from other organizations as distinct and unique. One activity I ask leaders to do is keep their core values on an easy-to-view document near their desks and refer to them often when making decisions and crafting communication.
- **Lead by Example.** Leaders set the tone by embodying the values and behaviors they want to see in their teams. There is a CEO who speaks about values in just about every internal talk he gives and in meetings, including those with customers. His dedication and commitment to values is a best practice I share with clients who are seeking to develop a positive culture. Although this might seem redundant, you can't over-emphasize the importance of reinforcing your values and communicating your vision and mission to connect people to the purpose. Leading by example is how you demonstrate these values in everything you do and say to model the desired culture of the organization.
- **Foster Belonging.** Strong cultures embrace diversity while also fostering a sense of belonging. You see this developed in the military and on sports teams. People might be diverse as individuals, yet they come together at work for a common purpose. Great teams support one another through winning and losing. They respect and value each person's contribution but put the team above their individual success.
- **Empower People.** How you empower and assign authority dictates the culture you create. That's not to say, however, that

everyone enjoys vast amounts of decision-making and little supervision. Some of us have autonomy as a higher core value than others. The culture of empowerment still requires processes and procedures, or you can't scale and create a system that drives ongoing great experiences for your employees and customers. Find ways to give team members input and they will feel more empowered. Just like we now want our coffee at Starbucks consistently made how we like it, we also want consistency in the direction we receive at work. Empowerment and consistency work together.

- **Provide Growth and Development Opportunities.** When organizations support personal and professional growth by providing training, mentoring, and opportunities for advancement, they not only ensure employees are more competent in their roles, but also set the tone for the organizational culture as one that is focused on developing people. Contrary to what I hear from leaders who refuse to develop employees for fear they may leave after, the vast majority become more contributing members and loyal. Watch out for talent hoarders or those who avoid developing team members. These behaviors will derail your efforts to create a culture where employees want to stay.
- **Design Reward Systems Around Culture.** Our reward, incentive, and recognition programs are part of the culture. If an organization has a culture problem, I always investigate incentives to understand if how they are incentivizing could be part of it. One instance where I saw incentives harm cultures and the customer experience was with car dealerships.

  Years ago, salespeople were paid commissions based on sales, which drove a high-pressure, individualistic culture. Then, many dealerships included customer satisfaction and only paid full commission on 5-star ratings, so some salespeople began hyper-pressuring customers to rate them a perfect score. This happened to me multiple times, and unfortunately, the dealership didn't get valuable feedback because they penalized salespeople for anything below perfection. This practice provided an opening for companies like Carvana, where you can avoid dealerships and salespeople altogether.

- **Promote Collaboration & Teamwork.** Another action toward creating a positive culture is to encourage collaboration and teamwork. Some executives believe crafting a culture that reinforces individual contributions brings out the best in everyone through competition. However, I have worked in and with cultures like this, and you reduce your talent pool because few people enjoy this "Survivor" type of culture. You also stunt innovation because one person's idea working alone rarely succeeds. When we have cultures that leverage our diverse teams working together, we can adapt and change more rapidly to meet the challenges of an uncertain future.

After defining and developing a positive work culture within the Leaders SUCCEED together© system, the final step is to sustain the culture you have worked hard to create.

3. Sustain

Defining and developing a positive work culture is not a one-time effort—it requires ongoing, intentional work, commitment, and sustainability from leaders. Here are some actionable strategies leaders can use to succeed at sustaining a positive culture:

- **Be Intentional.** Of course, this is repeated from above, but only because I cannot say it enough. Intentional leaders don't just live within the existing culture and take for granted that it will continue. Instead, they choose each day to create and sustain it.

- **Continuous Feedback.** Cultural assessment, creation, and sustainment is an ongoing loop. As your organization grows, people come and go, and competitive forces create new opportunities for innovation. Consequently, your culture may shift and change. To sustain a positive culture means maintaining a feedback loop with employees to monitor the culture's health.
- **Encourage Career Pathing.** Sustaining a positive work culture takes intention and feedback. It also requires designing career paths demonstrating the organization is committed to ongoing growth. Organizations that provide development that meets the needs of new generations coming into the workplace have an opportunity to create an employer brand-of-choice and a workforce ready for the future ahead.
- **Address Issues Promptly.** Just like waiting too long to go to the doctor with symptoms of illness can have adverse consequences, ignoring the signs that something is amiss in our culture can have consequences too. Using the skills we learned in the communication section will provide us with the tools to minimize conflict and promote collaboration to sustain a positive work culture.
- **Continuously Evolve and Improve.** A culture that can evolve is more likely to remain positive. Leaders can embrace this sense of evolution by being flexible and adaptive in response to changing circumstances, whether industry trends, technological advancements, or global events. Changing with customers' and clients' needs will win in the marketplace against competitors who miss the mark on intentionally designing culture.

Defining, developing, and sustaining a positive work culture is a multi-faceted journey that requires strong leadership and ongoing commitment. Leaders play a pivotal role in creating culture.

Ultimately, a positive work culture is not just achieving a goal, but an ongoing process that benefits everyone within the organization because these are places where team members can become the very best versions of themselves.

Chapter Summary

Great leaders effectively cultivate and sustain a positive work culture. Like soil influences the quality of the plants that can grow, a toxic or healthy culture can do the same for the people in a work environment. By using the Leaders SUCCEED together© system, focusing on culture, leaders can create a competitive advantage by intentionally defining, developing, and sustaining their work cultures.

- **Understanding Culture.** Culture in an organization is akin to its personality, shaped by shared beliefs, values, attitudes, and practices. It's a complex set of values and beliefs that dictate how an organization operates and interacts, and leaders play a vital role in shaping and evolving this culture.
- **Three Components of Culture in the Leaders SUCCEED together© System:**
    1. **Define.** Conduct employee surveys, observational analysis, focus groups, and policy reviews to define the existing culture. Look for discrepancies between stated values and actual practices. Understand that culture can manifest differently across various organizational levels and locations.
    2. **Develop.** Define core values and lead by example to embody them. Foster a sense of belonging and empower team members to contribute. Offer growth and development opportunities. Design reward systems that align with the desired culture. Promote collaboration and teamwork to enhance the collective spirit.

3. **Sustain.** Be intentional in actions and decisions that impact culture. Implement a continuous feedback loop for ongoing cultural assessment. Encourage career pathing to show commitment to employee growth. Address cultural issues promptly and effectively. Continuously evolve and adapt the culture in response to internal and external changes.

Successful leaders are intentional in their actions and decisions, while constantly engaging with their teams and actively assessing and evolving the culture to ensure it remains healthy and positive. This commitment to culture benefits the employees and contributes to the organization's overall success and competitiveness.

By following the Leaders SUCCEED together© system, leaders have the tools they need to create a thriving organizational environment and competitive advantage that is difficult to replicate.

Now, let's Do, Reflect, and Discuss how we will apply these learnings before we move forward.

Do

1. Identify signs, symbols, and language that describe your organization's culture. If you are starting a company, what do you want your company culture to be?
2. Refer to the list of ways organizations develop positive work cultures and categorize where your current culture is doing well and where your current work culture could improve.
3. Read this list of ways to sustain a positive work culture and identify areas where you are doing well and where there could be improvement.

Reflect

1. If your organization was a person, how would you describe their

personality?
2. How is the culture within your team? Are there areas where you could improve?
3. What specific things could you do to improve your workplace culture?

Discuss

1. Describe the culture at your workplace and what signs, symbols, and language point to that culture.
2. Share about a time when you have worked in a toxic culture or very positive culture and how it made you feel. How was performance influenced?
3. Discuss specific ideas to develop and sustain a positive work culture.

Chapter 6: Expectations

The Leadership Compass

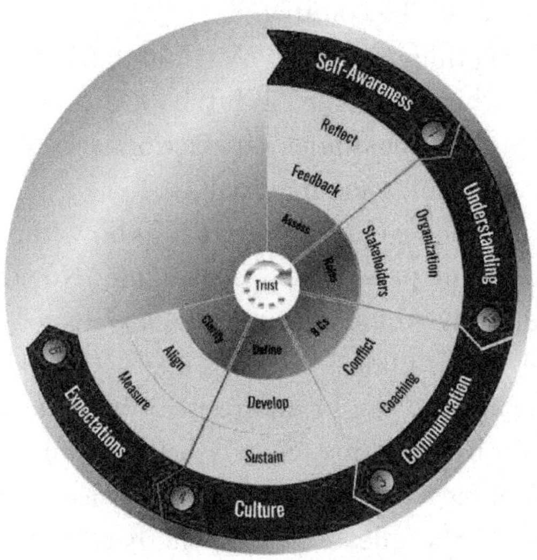

I believe that, with a few exceptions, people want to come to work and succeed. We have a desire to achieve expectations and feel like we are accomplishing great work. However, sometimes those expectations are not clear, and we find ourselves in a maze, trying to figure it out on our own. Other times, if we know where we are headed and have a leader to guide us along the way, it can be one of the most exciting journeys of our careers.

Here's one of the most challenging and fun roles I have held and how it got me hooked on building things.

In the early 90's, I was hired by a small, privately held bank by the owner's son. He thought I had an innovative spirit, and we seemed to share a vision that banking could be a much better experience for customers.

At the time he had a small group of people answering phones (Literally picking up corded phones). They didn't have a call center like other banks. He set forth the challenge that I would build him a state-of-the-art call center in one year. But he also supported me in sending me all over the country to meet with experts and tour the best contact centers in the country.

I learned everything I could. We found the best technology, designed the right hiring profile, built the location, and began taking calls within a year. The customer satisfaction was over 90%, and we won a national tele-professional award.

During that time, we began noticing how the internet was expanding. Many bank presidents were saying, "No one will ever use this www thing. Why would anyone need a website? No intelligent human will ever bank online."

However, he and I thought differently. We believed that people would eventually bank online. Slowly, other banks started to use some online banking. Our customer base was heavily weighted toward retirees, so the question was whether they would adapt. I believed they could if we made it easy enough to use.

He set a second expectation and asked me to build him an online banking center. I worked in the basement of the bank with outside Microsoft programmers he hired to design screens, and we finally launched in under than a year. (Despite every executive in the bank calling me an idiot who was wasting company money.)

Again, my leader set the expectation and allowed me to do what I needed to make it happen, which included a great team of leaders who worked with me to achieve our goals. The day we received our first $200K online deposit I went down to the president's office (his father) and set it on his desk. He shook his head and said, "Now I need you to build me a mortgage contact center." That was another success which led me to realize that building is what I do best.

You see, when we're clear about expectations, we can bring out the best in our leaders. During that time, by building and working together with a great team, I also achieved my personal goal to become the VP of a bank before I was 30 years old.

The future of AI excites me because I see so many possibilities. Sure, there will be bad things that come from it as well, just like the dark web emerged, but overall, these new technologies will create opportunities for people and organizations to achieve more than they thought possible and thrive.

Where are we headed, and how will we know when we have arrived? Just like many hikers use a compass to identify the way forward when cell service is spotty, leaders are responsible for identifying where the team is today, and where they are going. A little celebration when you arrive doesn't hurt, either!

Just like hikers who scale mountains prepare for the journey, setting and achieving performance expectations is a core responsibility for leaders who want to succeed and help others to become the best they can be.

Ripple Effects of Expectations

I see this often in organizations: When one group doesn't set and achieve performance expectations, it has a ripple effect throughout the organization.

For example, suppose one department doesn't establish clear expectations and achieve its goals. In that case, other departments must compensate for the poor performance since the company has to meet its financial objectives or risk being unable to stay in business. It also creates tension and potential animosity between teams because people notice when one person or group is not pulling their weight.

As leaders who succeed, we inspire and create trusting relationships that ultimately lead people toward becoming the best version of themselves and that contribute to the organization's success. Just like people who don't set expectations or goals to focus on their performance, organizations that lose track of performance end up not living up to their potential.

Here are three examples of leaders known for managing performance expectations. As you read these, ask: "Do I agree with their approach?"

- **Jack Welch - General Electric**. Jack Welch, the former CEO of General Electric (GE), was renowned for his distinctive and effective approach to performance management. He implemented the "vitality curve" model, also known as "rank and yank," where employees were categorized into three groups: the top 20% (high performers), the middle 70% (average performers), and the bottom 10% (low performers). The bottom 10% were often let go. This controversial method was credited with significantly improving GE's profitability and operational efficiency during his tenure, but many question the longer-term impact. However, Welch's intended approach emphasized the importance of clear performance metrics, accountability, and the need for continuous improvement within an organization.
- **Satya Nadella – Microsoft.** Satya Nadella, CEO of Microsoft, is recognized for transforming Microsoft's culture and performance management system. Under his leadership, Microsoft shifted from a culture of internal competition to one focused on collaboration, innovation, and a growth mindset. Nadella introduced more flexible and frequent performance check-ins, moving away from the traditional annual review system. This approach placed a stronger emphasis on employee learning and development, fostering a more supportive and productive work environment. Nadella's leadership significantly

improved employee morale and led to impressive business results for Microsoft.

- **Anne Mulcahy – Xerox.** Anne Mulcahy, the former CEO of Xerox, is celebrated for her role in turning around the company's fortunes. Faced with the threat of bankruptcy, Mulcahy focused on rigorous performance management to drive recovery. She prioritized transparency in communication, setting clear and achievable targets for employees at all levels. Mulcahy emphasized the importance of customer relations and innovation as key performance indicators. Under her leadership, Xerox shifted its focus from short-term financial gains to long-term sustainability and growth, emphasizing effective cost management, quality improvement, and customer satisfaction. Mulcahy's strategic focus on performance management helped Xerox regain its position as a leader in the document management industry.

You can see that different approaches to managing performance expectations can work well. As with everything in the world, as we learn more, we have an opportunity to reflect and change. We now know that Malachy's and Nadella's approaches have a better overall impact on culture than the GE method.

Yet, I still see some organizations behind the curve using stacked ranking. The Leaders SUCCEED together© system encourages ongoing learning and development because people and our world change, and as leaders we can expand the impact we make by being flexible and adaptive.

When leaders clarify, align, and measure performance expectations, they find that teams are more motivated to succeed. But don't forget to make sure that any expectations you're setting align with your organizational vision, mission, and values.

That's why the Leaders SUCCEED together© system includes three steps to managing performance expectations: 1. Clarify, 2.

Align, and 3. Measure, which are critical for leaders if they want to exceed performance expectations.

1. Clarify

No one wants to come to work and fail. Most people enjoy feeling like they're succeeding at their jobs. However, we still have underperforming team members who may or may not know it.

I have had many coaching clients tell me they don't know what their boss wants from them from one day to the next. It's no wonder so many new leaders fail. Some organizations spend months or weeks and significant cost to interview and hire people, but then fail to onboard them in a way that clarifies what they are specifically responsible for.

Many clients explain that they're in an ongoing maze to discover what they are expected to do and achieve because their leader constantly changes their minds. The good news is that, as a coach, with the client's permission, I can sit down with their leader and get a clear list of what success looks like in their mind. For anyone without a coach, I advise you to work to pinpoint your leader's expectations.

If you're an entrepreneur or the CEO, consider if the people on your team are clear about expectations. Many leaders believe their team members should know what they were hired to do. But even if you think you know, it's best to check for understanding continually.

Successful leaders clarify performance expectations by ensuring job descriptions, discussions, and goals are clear for each team member. This drives engagement, which we will discuss in the next chapter.

- **Job Descriptions.** As we discussed in Chapter 2, knowing what we are responsible for doing at work is critical to feeling motivated and like we can succeed. For large organizations, job descriptions outlining detailed responsibilities are expected. For smaller organizations or startups, these may need to be created, maintained, and updated as the company grows. It's an excellent yearly process to review everyone's job description and determine if any updates or changes need to be made. I can't tell you how many times I've taken over departments and none of the job descriptions were accurate. This doesn't mean that team members should not go outside of these descriptions. It just means everyone has a roadmap they can follow.

- **Discussions.** In addition to job descriptions, frequent discussions can help ensure everyone understands what they are responsible for doing in their roles. A lack of role clarity is a key contributor to low performance and engagement. This doesn't mean micro-managing, but it does mean being on the same page about what and how each person contributes to the work that needs to be done.

  It's also important to clarify within and between teams who is responsible for what activities. There is so much conflict and disengagement caused by a lack of role clarity that it always seems to come up in my consulting practice and workshops. It is one of the places where time, energy, and resources are wasted because we don't establish clear roles and responsibilities. It's probably why people use the term 'swim lanes' when allocating project work. Can you imagine a swim meet without any lanes and swimmers swimming all over the pool? It would be chaos, which is what some teams I work with are like. Not knowing who is supposed to be doing what causes so much frustration.

  A tool like a RACI chart has been successful for many clients to assign who is responsible, accountable, consulted, and informed. This type of system is usually reserved for project managers, but clients from all industries can benefit if role clarity is the issue. Of course, you don't have to delineate every single task. Still, if everyone owns it, no one owns it, so making sure everyone knows who is ultimately accountable, even if the entire team has responsibility, will help improve the chance that you will meet and exceed expectations.

- **Goal Setting.** I have always had my team members set yearly goals and create initiatives under each goal that will be done throughout the year so they can see how their goals are going to be met. Some leaders prefer monthly or quarterly goal setting. Whichever works best for your company, the most important part is having clear performance expectations connected to goals. The SMART goal framework has many forms, but generally, it ensures goals are specific, measurable, achievable, realistic, and time-bound. Sadly, I've had several clients who cannot articulate their goals, and they're typically underperformers, according to their leaders. Unfortunately, their leader owns some of the blame because working with team members to clarify goals is the leader's responsibility.

  - **Communication.** I know we took time to discuss communication in the earlier chapter. However, clarifying expectations and goals requires communication, so I want to reinforce it. I've seen many employees struggle trying to figure out how and when their leader wants them to communicate about progress, performance, etc., and not ask. This is especially true for team members just joining the workforce. Give them some grace, please, and let's all remember when we were new at work. With the modes of communication shifting, you may communicate via text, Teams, Slack, email, phone calls, meetings, and who knows what other ways will be possible by the time this book is published.

One misstep that I find, especially when leaders move into the role for the first time, is clarifying how and what is to be communicated. For instance, I had a leader whose boss became furious when he didn't call him over the weekend to alert him that a shipment would not go out to a key client. In the person's defense, he had no idea that this was the appropriate protocol and was respecting his manager's time at home. I've had other leaders frustrated by text messages from team members when they would have preferred the information sent via email, and still others upset that they received an email and not a text message.

Our method and communication modes become part of the culture we create, and as we discussed, sometimes it takes a while to figure out the culture. So, if we remember to clarify the communication expectations with our team members, we can support them in meeting and exceeding our expectations. Some leaders claim that communication expectations develop naturally as people begin working with one another. However, it's best to be up front about how to best communicate with you. Even when it comes to how to communicate with so many channels at our fingertips.

For instance, people who work with me know that my home and work life are integrated by choice. My husband and I have both worked from home for years and traveled with our jobs, so we choose that integration in a way that works for us and our family. That means you will see my emails at all hours and on weekends. In my last organizational leadership role, I realized team members were responding almost immediately to every request I had over the weekend, and I became very concerned. I knew I had to clarify with my team that just because they see an email from me on the weekend or after regular business hours, it doesn't mean that I expect a response during that time. Emails are fine to respond to the next workday.

However, if I text or call you after hours, you can assume it is an emergency, so please do your best to contact me. I could see the relief in some of their faces, and one of my team members said that she was feeling burned out and overwhelmed because I sent notes on the evenings and weekends. Going forward, I tried to delay my emails to her until work hours. Still, many of my other team members also practice work/life integration as I do, so they like receiving emails when I send them so they can respond when they have a moment in the evening or weekend and don't have something waiting on them the next business day. Again, it's about clarifying expectations from both a performance and how-we-get-our-work-done perspective that will help you succeed.

- **Caution on Goal Setting.** I have worked with many leaders who believe in BHAG (Big, Hairy, Audacious Goals). Although I do believe in setting aggressive goals, going too far above what is realistic can become demotivating and work counter to your objectives as a leader to move performance forward. There are many methods for goal setting, but whatever you do, include the team members in the process and ensure that the goals you set are reasonable enough that they can be achieved. Otherwise, you risk creating a negative culture and demotivating some of your best people.

  For instance, I remember a leader who consistently set goals for his team that were 50% higher than what he committed to his corporate office. I always set a higher forecast than the budget to make sure we met our financial commitments. However, this leader took it even further by not telling his team that the baseline budget was 50% lower than the goal he set for them. He also didn't work with his team to produce a way forward as to how they could achieve the goal. Three months into the year, the team gave up, and although they met the forecast, he ended up losing many leaders who felt demotivated. Goal setting is an art and a science, so balance exceeding performance expectations and keeping your team motivated.

As we help our team members know the expectations and how they are responsible for doing their work, we also want to ensure everyone understands how their work and goals align with the organization to increase motivation, which is the next step in the Leaders SUCCEED together© system for exceeding expectations.

2. Align

Successful leaders work to align performance goals with the broader vision and mission of the organization and adjust if needed. Communication is critical here because people want to be part of something bigger than themselves, and it's our job as leaders to help them see how that is possible.

I heard an executive talk recently about visiting a medical manufacturing facility. There, he observed posters of doctors using the medical devices they were making throughout various work areas in the plant.

Smiling patients and doctors who benefited from some of the applications were visual communications of how their work contributed not only to the product, but to improving the lives of people they could see on the posters. This plant was higher performing than the others, and this alignment of their work with the patient outcomes was the one notable difference.

As discussed in the earlier chapter on culture, people want to understand how their work contributes to a meaningful output. We all want purpose and meaning in our lives, so aligning individual roles with strategic objectives within the organization focused on achieving high performance is critical for leaders.

From the lowest to the highest level of the organization, people need to understand how all the puzzle pieces fit together, not to mention across the organization. When I work with companies, I hear consistently about silos creating barriers to performance.

Aligning performance expectations, roles, responsibilities, and goal setting across the organization in ways that people understand how resources are divided and shared can be a real difference maker for your organization.

One client shared that after clarifying job descriptions, roles, responsibilities, and goal setting, she heard from some employees that they were enjoying the sense of accomplishment they felt when they knew more clearly what they were expected to do and their goals.

However, there was still significant conflict between departments, especially with her sales and operations team. There were even conflicts impacting performance with departments that reported to her, and she found that most of it stemmed from misaligned goals.

Operations was accountable for holding zero inventory, while sales were responsible for meeting customer product demand. Backlogs and missed shipments were constant. She found that conflicting goals and metrics also inhibited performance within her departments.

For the areas where she was directly responsible, she brought the key leaders together and asked them to propose goals that aligned with one another. Outside of her area, she spoke with the sales leader, and together, they proposed an update to both of their goals that would create alignment. She then took the time to develop a strategy presentation that she shared with her team and every employee of the site location that explained how the goals for each person rolled up to the teams, and the teams to the site, and the site's contribution to the organization.

Throughout the presentation, she also told stories of end-users who were positively impacted by the products they were making. You wouldn't believe the transformation in both employee engagement and customer satisfaction—all by aligning expectations!

Another area related to aligning expectations for teams is projects. I think most of us who have spent time in the workforce have seen projects derailed, looking like train wrecks. I was conducting a virtual leadership development program, and the participants shared that they had difficulty meeting their project goals because teams weren't aligned on who was responsible for what outcome.

With everyone working across the globe, they also didn't have alignment on what times they could have meetings, so many key members missed meetings because they were held during their off hours. This type of misalignment between teams can mean the difference between success and failure. This is why clarifying and aligning expectations, not only for team members, but for teams and within and between departments, will improve the chances of success for the entire organization.

Aligning our work within the organization with internal stakeholders and customers allows us to feel part of something larger than ourselves, which makes work meaningful. But just like no sport is played without a scoreboard, the next step in the Leaders SUCCEED together© system is to make sure you are measuring what matters.

3. Measure

It's been said that what gets measured gets managed. I know when I want to lose weight, avoiding the scale is not an option. I need to know where I am today, my progress, and my trends to achieve my goals. Can you imagine watching a basketball or football game without a scoreboard? Not only would that not be very fun, but it also wouldn't be very motivating for the players if they knew no one was keeping score of their achievements.

- **Reporting & Scorecards.** In many organizations, real-time or daily scorecards and systems track metrics that matter, and this works well. The key is measuring those metrics that matter to your organization and keeping the list manageable.
  For instance, there was one client I was working with to improve sales and service within their contact centers, and I asked them which metrics they were tracking. In my email, I received a spreadsheet with 200 lines of data.
  As someone who loves a great spreadsheet and can't get enough data, I was thrilled they could track and report on so much information. And then I asked a follow-up question. "So which ones of these are you showing your leaders and team members each day?" The response was concerning. Their VP smiled proudly and said, "All of them. We track, monitor, and report on 200 data points daily." As the smile from seeing the comprehensive spreadsheet left my face, I thought, *Oh no. Now I know exactly why their teams are not performing. They are buried in information.* I observed their daily cross-site calls. Leaders were asked about the 200 metrics, with about half in the red on the Excel sheet for that day. There was no way they could be leading people if they were tracking down all those metrics, and it was clear that they were spending more time tracking data than working with people or improving their business. What this organization failed to do is clarify which metrics really mattered. They needed to clarify and report on the metrics that were in the control of the people in that location and connected directly to driving the performance expectations they needed to achieve through their valuable team members. Although, in the background, it's great to have analytics and information on every aspect you can for your business, the human brain cannot process

and connect this many metrics to behaviors that drive performance. I recommended analyzing the most important metrics and selecting 3-5 to manage daily. Ultimately, for this client we settled on eight core metrics, a big improvement from leaders trying to manage 200 data points daily. This *one* change made a significant difference in getting the team rallied around what they were expected to achieve and improved performance across all the metrics.

- **Ongoing Updates.** Some organizations use daily huddles or weekly updates, especially for new or frontline team members. In healthcare and other environments, there are shift change meetings and daily huddles. At a minimum, I recommend weekly check-ins and more formalized monthly updates on progress and goals for department leaders to help prioritize and support teams without micro-managing.

  Here is how I discovered the power of monthly updates. I had just become a senior vice president responsible for sales results across seven sites. I realized that the scorecards and metrics were helpful, and I had them online and updated for everyone to see throughout each day. However, I also knew that leadership was more than management of metrics. Everyone had projects and other responsibilities within their roles. So, I implemented the monthly update process.

  Each of my leaders was required to send a monthly update before the fifth of the month highlighting four things: performance to goal, key initiatives with progress, anything I can do to help, along with focus areas for the next month. It was a simple four-point update that I requested to be one page.

  The one-page rule was later reinforced by one of my students who was in the military. He said they had a rule that all their report updates had to be one page. So much so that his commanding officer would throw away any report that had a staple. As the saying goes, I would have written you a shorter letter if I had more time.[24]

The first time I developed and used this process over a year, I was surprised at how easy and effective it made coaching sessions and year-end reviews. Not to mention accountability. In my organization at the time, we had to compete with many of our peers for bonus dollars for our teams by meeting and calibrating employee performance. I would come to the meeting with data from monthly reports that would back up my case for certain members of my team who I believed deserved more than the standard bonus.

Having data and specific examples to support my requests when many other leaders only used their general comments ensured my team was properly represented and earned the bonuses they deserved. Holding people accountable and having coaching conversations using these monthly updates was also much more straightforward.

When someone writes that they are not making their goals, it allows you to help address the gap before it becomes an ongoing trend. The other benefit of monthly updates is having your leaders report monthly to one another. I have had clients change to this process and they see immediate results in collaboration and communication. Ongoing updates on performance expectations help tie everyone together toward thinking about new ways to achieve goals.

When Performance Expectations Are Not Met

In my consulting practice, this topic comes up a lot. Whether I'm working with a business owner on their organizational strategy or coaching a client from just about anywhere, dealing with situations where people are not meeting performance expectations can be a challenge.

As I mentioned at the start of the chapter, people don't want to fail, and they don't like to have team members who are failing. As a leader, if you have clarified, aligned, and measured expectations and coached the person appropriately, there will still be times when people will not achieve the performance they need to succeed.

Once you have done everything you can to support them, it may be time to invite them to find a position outside the company. I say this nicely because we want to treat people with respect, and off boarding team members with care is an opportunity to demonstrate that we value and respect people—even during difficult circumstances.

Sadly, throughout my career, I have had to reduce hundreds of jobs at different times due to economic situations where the business wasn't meeting expectations. I've had to let many leaders go on to find other roles because they weren't successful in the position I hired them for. These are never easy conversations and decisions, but once you talk with your HR business partner, if you have one, it's best not to delay.

Allowing one team member not to achieve their goals sets the tone for everyone else, and it can create cracks in the type of high-performing culture you want to achieve. Seek counsel from legal, HR, or other leaders as needed, but then do what needs to be done so that you can allow that person to find a place and role where they can succeed.

Cautions for Managing Performance Expectations

Unfortunately, implementing processes at the end of the year—like forced stacked ranking employees—endeavors to address a fundamental issue of managers not accurately measuring performance. Pitting team members against one another and forcing leaders to create an imaginary bell curve can be detrimental to organizational performance and employee morale.

When I was forced to do stack ranking that required me to rank a performing team member as not performing, it was one of the reasons I left an organization I enjoyed. The research about the detrimental effects of this practice hadn't caught up yet, but we know now what I kept saying back then: Forced stack ranking encourages a myriad of destructive behaviors and can decimate cultures. Avoid it at all costs.

Here are two other examples of how managing performance can go wrong:

- Uber faced numerous controversies related to its workplace culture, including allegations of harassment and discrimination. The organization's performance management system was criticized for not effectively addressing and mitigating such issues, ultimately affecting employee morale and public image.
- Wells Fargo also faced a scandal in 2016 when it was discovered that employees had opened millions of unauthorized customer accounts to meet ambitious sales targets. The company's intense sales-oriented performance management system was identified as a significant contributing factor to this unethical behavior. Both situations illustrate that even in large, well-established firms, taking our eyes off managing performance expectations can effectively impact our organizations substantially.

Whether you're a private, public, or non-profit organization, you must achieve your performance expectations. Shareholders, team members, owners, patients, students, donors, and other stakeholders count on your organization to survive and thrive. By clarifying, aligning, and measuring performance expectations, leaders will achieve their goals and develop other leaders who know how to succeed.

Chapter Summary

Leaders play a critical role in managing performance to meet and exceed organizational expectations. Just like a compass can tell us where we are right now and show us how to move in the direction we want to travel, leading performance expectations sets the path forward. When we create trusting and inspiring relationships with team members by clarifying, aligning, and measuring within the Leaders SUCCEED together© system, everyone can become their best.

- **Performance Management Examples.** Jack Welch at General Electric, Satya Nadella at Microsoft, and Anne Mulcahy at Xerox had different approaches to managing performance expectations. While Welch's "vitality curve" approach and its controversial nature are explored. Nadella's emphasis on collaboration and Mulcahy's focus on transparency and long-term sustainability are highlighted as transformative leadership styles.
- **Three Components of Expectations in the Leaders SUCCEED together© system:**
  1. **Clarify.** Emphasizes the importance of clear job descriptions, regular discussions, goal setting, and effective communication. When leaders ensure team members are aware of their responsibilities and how to accomplish them, they have the framework for success.
  2. **Align.** Aligning individual goals with the organization's vision and mission will bring out the best in people and set the organization up for success. Misalignment, however, can lead to internal conflicts and reduced performance.
  3. **Measure.** Like checking your GPS to make sure you are on the right route, establishing appropriate metrics and regular

updates will keep you on track. Scorecards and providing ongoing feedback to ensure teams are aware of their progress will keep the team motivated.

Sometimes expectations are not met, and even as hard as we try as leaders, we can't avoid having to make a change. The importance of respectful off boarding and maintaining a high-performance culture are also key roles of leaders.

- **Pitfalls in Performance Management.** There are many pitfalls in performance management systems, such as the cases of Uber and Wells Fargo, which illustrate how leadership decisions detrimentally impact employee morale and could unintentionally lead to unethical practices.

Overall, when we clarify, align, and measure expectations, we have an opportunity to set our team members up for achieving success many of them never dreamed possible.

Now, let's Do, Reflect, and Discuss performance expectations to become the leaders we were meant to be and support others in also becoming the best version of themselves.

Do

1. Review how you performed last year according to your goals and how you are currently doing this year.
2. Match your performance expectations and those of your team with your organization's overall goals and strategy.
3. Create a plan for you to clarify, align, and measure performance more effectively on your team.

Reflect

1. Where are you exceeding, meeting, or not meeting performance expectations? What about each of your team members?

2. How do the performance expectations you have set for yourself, and others align with your organization? How might this alignment be clarified or improved?
3. Think about one person who is struggling with performance and how you can better support them in achieving their goals.

Discuss

1. Share how your organization manages performance expectations. Do you believe this process is effective?
2. Which leader discussed in the chapter, Jack Welch, Satya Nadella, and Anne Mulcahy, had the best approach for managing performance?
3. How has the generational shifts impacted the way we manage performance? Are there generational or cultural differences in how we manage performance?

Chapter 7: Engagement

The Leadership Spark

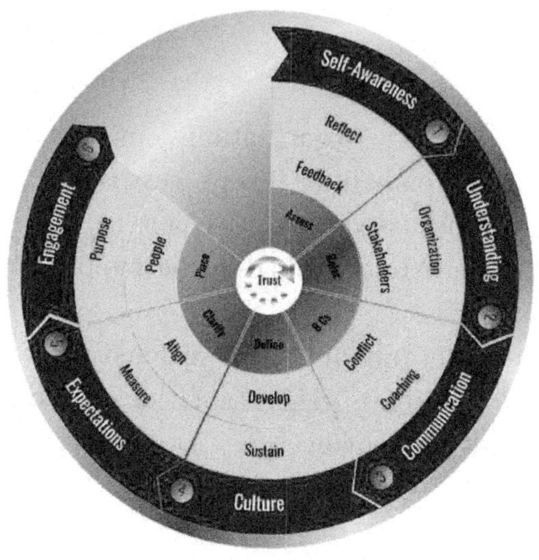

I was serving as a fractional chief marketing officer and researcher for one of my clients, and I had just completed an analysis of the employee engagement survey results for them. It was this day when I saw how one leader could impact engagement. We had been conducting the survey for five years, and this client amazed me by consistently having over 90% employee satisfaction and engagement indicators across categories extremely high.

The CEO was friendly and enthusiastic, and the leaders throughout the organization were intelligent, driven, and positive. This year, however, the results were terrible. The employee satisfaction was only 48%, which is extremely low, and engagement indicators across the board were lower than ever. I analyzed the data and then began to analyze the comments. Something major had changed.

Normally when I see such drastic changes, it is due to massive layoffs, mergers, or something else specifically. But I checked in with the organization and none of that was happening. The comments started pointing to someone newly being hired who was being described as very different from other leaders. The name wasn't directly mentioned, and from the comments made, I could see that a sense of fear of repercussions had been instilled in the team.

I really liked the CEO and hated to be the bearer of bad news, because I know he takes his team engagement seriously. However, as a researcher, I was dying of curiosity to know who this person was and how they could impact the organization within just a year—albeit negatively.

We began the conference call, and I introduced myself. The executives introduced themselves and a woman named Anna said she was the new COO who had just been hired in the last year. As I started the presentation, she said, "OK, everyone. Let's see what these big babies are whining about now. I bet they're sad we took their lollipops away and are making them work."

I am really glad it was a phone conference without video, because I could never have hidden the look on my face. It was Anna! She had singlehandedly cut employee engagement down by about half.

For the rest of the presentation, she discounted what the team members said, and although the CEO was soft spoken, I could hear the disappointment in his voice.

Within three months I heard Anna *had found* another opportunity outside of the company. The next year the results began to trend up. Yes, just one leader can influence engagement for everyone around them. You get to decide if you will be the one who brings engagement up or down.

Have you ever worked in a role or workplace where you couldn't wait to get to work? Somewhere that the excitement and energy you felt while working together toward a common goal was contagious? Conversely, have you ever hoped that you would come down with the flu rather than go to work? Or have you worked in a place that was so draining you couldn't wait to go home?

Those around us influence how we feel about work. If we can master the skill of driving engagement, it can be the spark that ignites an excitement for achieving great work within an organization. It also gives us the power to retain the most talented workforce and become a competitive advantage.

Why Employee Engagement?

Most of us have heard about employee engagement. Gallup defines employee engagement as the involvement and enthusiasm of employees in both their work and workplace.[25]

In their recent State of the Global Workplace report, Gallup found that 23% of the workforce is thriving, 59% are quiet quitting (or disengaged), and 18% are loud quitting (actively disengaged), costing the global economy an estimated $8.8 trillion—9% of global GDP.[26]

Most research suggests that the direct leader (CEO, manager, or supervisor) has significant control over these results. That's why engagement has been embedded in the Leaders SUCCEED together© system—because you have the opportunity to make a difference as a leader every single day!

But before you think about those you lead, have you ever considered questions like, "Am I engaged in this work?" As leaders, we set the tone for everyone around us. Emotions are contagious, and how we show up for work each day matters. Leaders have the responsibility to engage themselves and everyone around them.

Even though it can be hard at times to come to work and be the best version of ourselves, we owe it to our teams and everyone around us to work toward staying engaged so we can engage others at work.

Another definition researchers have adopted for employee engagement refers to employees' emotional and psychological commitment toward their work, organizations, and goals. When I first became a manager, some higher-level leaders told me that all employees needed to leave their emotions at the door. What I didn't know then is that that's like asking someone to cut off their arm and leave it outside. We are integrated human beings, and it isn't possible, nor advisable, to ask team members not to bring their entire selves to work.

How much we share about our lives and our silent stories is our choice. Using self-awareness, understanding, and communication, we can lead ourselves better. Regardless of how we feel, when we remember that our emotions are contagious, and they influence everyone around us, we can choose the impact we have on other people.

As leaders, we want every team member to be engaged, meaning, they are deeply invested in their work, motivated to contribute their best efforts, and feel fulfilled and connected to their workplace. These are the people we want on our team because they are more likely to go the extra mile, exhibit high levels of job satisfaction, and actively contribute to the organization's success.[27]

From an organizational perspective, research has also found employee engagement leads to significant benefits. For example:

- **Increased Productivity and Performance**. Engaged employees tend to be more productive, resulting in enhanced organizational performance.
- **Improved Retention and Reduced Turnover**. Engaged employees are less likely to leave their organizations, reducing

turnover costs. One Gallup study calculates that engaged employees are 59% less likely to look for a job elsewhere within the next 12 months.[28]

- **Enhanced Employee Well-being**. Engaged employees experience higher levels of job satisfaction and overall well-being. Researchers have found that employee well-being significantly contributes to organizational success and is positively impacted by engagement.[29]
- **Improved Customer Satisfaction and Loyalty**. Engaged employees provide better customer service, leading to higher customer satisfaction and loyalty. Many researchers have found a direct link between employee engagement and customer satisfaction.
- **More Innovation and Creativity.** Engaged employees are more likely to contribute innovative ideas and engage in creative problem-solving. Other research highlights the positive relationship between employee engagement and creativity at work.[30]
- **Effective Change Management.** Engaged employees are more adaptable and receptive to organizational changes.[31]
- **Positive Organizational Culture**. Research suggests that engaged employees create a positive culture that, in turn, creates more engaged employees.[32]
- **Financial Impact**. Engaged employees positively impact an organization's financial performance.

Leaders play a pivotal role in fostering employee engagement by creating a supportive work environment, providing growth opportunities, offering meaningful work, and facilitating open communication. These efforts not only benefit employees, but also contribute to the overall success and sustainability of the organization.[33]

Leaders who create positive work cultures, develop employees, and ensure expectations are clear will see engagement improvement, which we discussed in earlier chapters.

For this chapter, I will focus on building connections within three areas we haven't yet covered in the Leaders SUCCEED together© system, all of which positively impact engagement: 1. Place, 2. People and 3. Purpose.

1. Place

Everyone wants to feel like they belong. I remember the comedy "Cheers" from the 1980's, where everyone in the bar yelled, "Norm!", one of the characters' names, whenever he entered the bar. The show's theme was about having a place to go where everyone knows your name.

Doesn't it feel good when someone greets you by name? Introverts and extroverts alike, we all want to be known and accepted by other people. It's an innate drive that has helped our survival as humans drawn to seeking protection in tribes. As leaders, our ability to connect employees to their workplace fosters a sense of belonging, engagement, and motivation. Whether we are working in person, remotely, or hybrid, leaders play a crucial role in creating a sense of belonging within workplaces.

Through earlier chapters, we have talked about using self-awareness, understanding, communication, and culture to design work environments that can reside in just about any physical space. However, from a place perspective, I also want to reinforce why physical space is important to consider when designing organizations where employees thrive.

Let's say you walk into a theater, and you sit in your assigned seat. You are sitting there, and someone approaches you and says they would like your seat. You paid for that seat and have been sitting in it for 15 minutes, but they would like it. Most of us would not give up our seats. Many of us would not move from that chair, even if we didn't pay for it. That seat is ours, and we now own it. In our minds, we have already connected with it, and it has become 'mine.'

Our connection to place begins in the toddler stage when children understand the term 'mine' and pull a toy away from another child because they believe it's theirs. They have attached to a particular toy, and it has become *their* toy.

As adults, we attach to physical items and space. At work, we not only attach to organizations from a psychological perspective, but we also attach to physical space. This means how we connect to the culture at work can be related to psychological and physical space.

For instance, I once worked with a Philippines site that had high employee attrition. It was across the street from another site that had a similar set up and took the same types of phone calls, but it had lower attrition. Having traveled to various locations, I was sure I knew the answer to what was causing the employees to leave.

The site with higher attrition had run out of space for team members, so they were 'hoteling.' This meant that no one had an assigned workspace. When they came to work, they took whatever desk was available. It sounds efficient, right? This is when I learned that efficiency is sometimes the enemy of effectiveness.

After a few focus groups, it was clear that the people at the hoteling site felt less connected. Not only was it challenging to come to work and find a space, but they also couldn't develop relationships with the people around them like they could if they worked at the site where desks were permanently assigned—the lower attrition site. They didn't seem to have the same connection to the organization either.

With the growth of hybrid and remote work, hoteling has become very popular. It can work if the team member has a healthy psychological attachment to the organization and a workspace at home where they are connected and comfortable. However, I always encourage leaders to make sure that every employee feels that they have a place to work where they can attach themselves to feel more connected to the organization. If they are working remotely in their home, they should have a separate office space to create distance between their home and workplaces to improve their connection.

Another issue I have found that impacts engagement related to place was an organization's move to eliminate doors and open all the offices to improve collaboration. The research shows, however, that collaboration decreases in open workspaces. With so many virtual calls happening at once, people leave the office and either go home or go somewhere else in the building to avoid distractions.

To increase engagement, workspace design is a critical piece to consider as you focus on developing places for people to belong.

A Place to Belong Remotely

Working from home is a requirement of any role I consider. Technology has evolved to allow me to work best with a mixture of in-person meetings and working from home. My husband has always worked remotely in his career, and I have worked from home for most of mine. However, I also would not choose this arrangement if I were starting my career because of the mentoring experiences I would have missed out on had I not been in an office.

Given the benefits of leveraging talent over the global workforce, we have employers and team members embracing all types of work situations. But how do you connect people to a place they belong when they work remotely? It can still be done effectively by giving them the tools and technology they need to connect.

Teams, Zoom, Slack, or similar tools can create a sense of belonging, even when people don't share a physical space. I also recommend that if you provide remote options, employees should have designated office space to focus solely on work. That means having childcare for children while working.

Many of the harshest critics of working from home are extreme extroverts. They cannot imagine how the rest of us do our best work from home—alone. Other critics have witnessed employees trying to work while caring for a child or believe that people who work remotely cannot be trusted to stay on task.

If you have someone you don't trust to work unless you're watching them, they shouldn't be working for you or your organization anyway. With the current state of technology, many roles cannot be done remotely, so leaders must design workplaces based on what will best meet the needs of customers, clients, and employees.

Leaders play a critical role in shaping organizations where employees feel a profound sense of belonging, both in psychological and physical spaces. Crafting workplaces that foster this sense of connection to a place of belonging can be a significant competitive advantage.

Here is a little more about the strategies that drive engagement related to place:

- **Flexible Work Arrangements.** Allowing employees to choose their work settings, times, and methods while considering client or customer needs enhances commitment and productivity.
- **Thoughtful Office Design.** Balancing private and communal spaces in office design can foster both focus and collaboration.
- **Providing Essential Tools.** Equipping employees with necessary tools like laptops, phones, and software supports efficient work in various settings.

- **Open Dialogue on Work Preferences.** Engaging in discussions about preferred work environments and being willing to adapt can enhance employee satisfaction.
- **Personalization of Workspaces.** Encouraging employees to personalize their workspaces can help them feel more connected to their work environment.
- **Designated Collaboration Spaces for Remote Team.** Providing specific areas for remote or hybrid team members to collaborate in person can strengthen team dynamics.
- **Strategic Planning of In-Office Days.** Ensuring that designated in-office days for hybrid employees are used for actual in-person interactions rather than virtual meetings.
- **Data-Driven Workspace Improvements.** Utilize customer satisfaction and employee engagement data to identify and address areas for improvement in workspace design.

By implementing these strategies, leaders can create environments where employees feel genuinely connected to their workplace, leading to increased engagement, satisfaction, and productivity.

2. People

Some of my clients have said that leadership would be great if it weren't for the people. I have heard from others who don't necessarily love their organization or their job, but they stay because they like the people. People are at the heart of every organization, and even with the power of artificial intelligence, organizations wouldn't exist if it weren't for their people.

Our view of people impacts how we lead. Human Resources as a department has struggled with their name for a long time. That's because we are trying to demonstrate a more human approach to leadership, which is important because the upcoming generations demand it.

HR used to be called Personnel—not engaging. Then, it shifted to Human Resources—more human, but resources get used up. Now, many of these departments are moving toward using Human Capital—which demonstrates value but doesn't feel very personal.

Others are shifting to names like the Office of People and other creative ways to describe the commitment to people. Regardless of what HR is called, the idea is that we now should all be recognizing the value of our team members and how important it is to engage them.

This is why people is the next area of focus within the engagement step in the Leaders SUCCEED together© system. The people part of engagement is focused on creating deeper connections between people at work. It's that psychological connection between coworkers, peers, team members, clients, or customers.

We are relational beings, and research consistently finds that when people feel connected to others at work, they are more likely to feel like they belong. Belongingness is a core need for us as humans, so it should not be a surprise that it leads to increased engagement.

A client recently told me that work was getting too "peopley." I know it's not a word, but I understood what she meant. She was feeling over-connected because she was more of an ambivert and needed some space from her team interactions. However, in general, the connections to the people she worked with kept her engaged and satisfied in her job.

When you're working to design roles, consider the strengths of each individual and evaluate how you can improve the connection each person has to someone inside or outside the company. As an independent consultant, I choose the clients I work with and develop strong relationships. I don't need an office full of coworkers to go to because of the deep connections I feel with my clients. Many of these people even become good friends over the years.

Through my research on passion, which will be another book at some point, I found that many of the frontline employees I interviewed were most passionate about serving clients. They felt a deep connection to their customers, driving their engagement. Other people need to have a tribe of people at work. They are most engaged when they are part of a team working toward a shared vision and goal. Many clients have also told me that their work has become part of their family. They feel supported and connected to their leader, peers, and teams, which engage them.

One of the most difficult decisions I ever made was leaving my global banking role—because of the people. I was surrounded by such great people in every role I worked in over the years I was there, and these connections contributed largely to my engagement.

Here are a few practical ways to ensure you are creating the right connections between people to drive engagement:

- **Customer Connections.** Design the workspace with pictures of happy customers using your products or experiencing your services. Share testimonials about how your product or service helped someone. Stories are powerful, so share the success the organization is having in as much detail as possible.
- **Reward & Recognition.** Recognize and reward people who go above and beyond to serve internal or external customers. Provide opportunities for team members to recognize one another for their work and celebrate key milestones.
- **Volunteerism.** Sponsor volunteer activities to demonstrate your commitment to service to your community and allow employees time off to attend. These events serve as excellent bonding for the team members.

- **Job Design.** Provide autonomy to allow team members the opportunity to go above and beyond to serve a client or customer.
- **Innovative Teamwork.** Allow team members to work together to create innovative solutions. These projects geared toward innovation will require creativity and potentially lead to bonding.
- **Team Outings/Events.** Encourage team members to have lunch or attend other outings or events to create stronger bonds. When they can bring their significant other, that also increases connections. My husband and I have been fortunate to be awarded trips over the years by our companies based on our performance, and we were permitted to bring one another. It's amazing how grateful and connected you feel when you have an opportunity to meet your partners' work colleagues.

Words of Wisdom on Events and Disconnection

Although outside-of-work, team events can be highly effective in improving connections and increasing engagement, there are just a few cautions I need to mention that you should consider.

Recently, a friend told me about a company she joined that liked to go to happy hours every Friday and drink until late in the evening. Although highly talented, she began to feel like an outsider because she didn't participate in what became late-night drunken festivities because she (a) didn't drink, and (b) had a family to go home to. No surprise, she left the company after only a few months.

Another client also shared that she felt like she didn't belong within her healthcare organization because only certain people were invited to go to lunch. She was always left out of the email invitations.

Other clients have shared that they were omitted from essential meetings or left off email communications because they didn't socialize, which had just as detrimental an effect in severing their connection with people and engagement. As a leader, we can watch for actions that drive wedges between people. Of course, we can't control the natural social relationships that form, but we can create systems to develop connections.

For example, if we have social events with our teams, we are also responsible for maintaining professionalism where everyone feels comfortable. Offsites and social events can be very powerful. Just be careful when planning these so that everyone can participate.

Another client said that he was invited to a team event that was a very physical hiking activity, and he felt embarrassed because he could not be part of it due to medical issues. These considerations need to be in the mix to ensure we are creating positive connections that create a sense of belonging and not unintentionally dividing people.

3. Purpose

The third aspect of creating engagement using the Leaders SUCCEED together© system is to focus on purpose. Have you ever felt like your work connected you to something much bigger than you could accomplish on your own? Do you feel, right now, in your work that the purpose of your organization aligns with your own purpose? Let's begin this discussion by connecting to your purpose.

Your Purpose in Life

I often hear people question their own purpose as they consider engagement. If you feel disengaged at work, I suspect that your purpose may not be aligned with your organization or be unclear.

We've already talked about the importance of defining success for yourself, now it's time to make sure you have defined your purpose.

Many of my clients benefit from taking the time to realign and reevaluate their purpose. Some practice this quarterly, or at a minimum, yearly, as they do goal setting and planning. Setting this north star helps bring clarity and connection to everything you are doing at home and work.

Humans have searched for purpose and meaning in their lives since the beginning of time, so knowing your individual purpose before you connect to the organizations purpose is an important step. Rick Warren's book *The Purpose Driven Life* has sold over fifty million copies and is a great resource I recommend to clients who are open to books about faith.[34]

Here are two other frameworks that I find helpful for this activity:

- **Ikigai.** Ikigai is a Japanese concept that refers to one's reason for being or life purpose.[35] It is often represented at the intersection of four elements: what you love, what you are good at, what the world needs, and what you can be paid for. Finding your Ikigai means discovering a balance between these aspects, leading to satisfaction, fulfillment, and meaning in life. This concept emphasizes the importance of aligning one's passion, profession, vocation, and mission to achieve a well-rounded and fulfilling life.
- **Avodah.** For those of you who are spiritually centered, a friend of mine and management consultant, Vic Clesceri, developed an approach called Avodah, which means "work, worship, and service" in Hebrew. It is different from Ikigai because it focuses on joy, gifts, service, and trusting that provision will be granted.[36]

Connecting People to Purpose

Although some people you talk with at work will tell you that they just do what they do for a paycheck, it's rare to find people who don't want to be part of something much bigger than dollars in the bank account. For leaders to succeed, connecting people to the organization's purpose is a strategic move for several compelling reasons:

- **Enhanced Employee Engagement.** Team members who understand and align with the organization's purpose are more likely to be engaged and motivated. Engagement leads to higher productivity, better job satisfaction, and lower turnover rates.
- **Increased Sense of Meaning and Fulfillment.** Team members who see how their work contributes to a larger goal often experience more significant meaning and fulfillment in their roles. This sense of purpose can be a powerful motivator and morale booster.
- **Improved Performance and Innovation.** A clear understanding of the organization's purpose can inspire employees to contribute more creatively and effectively. It often leads to innovative thinking, as employees are more invested in the organization's success.
- **Stronger Team Cohesion and Collaboration.** Shared purpose fosters a sense of community and teamwork. Employees are more likely to collaborate effectively when they are working towards a common goal.
- **Better Customer Experience.** Team members connected to the organization's purpose often provide better customer service, as they understand the more significant impact of their interactions and strive to represent the company's values positively.
- **Resilience in Times of Change.** During times of uncertainty or change, a strong connection to the organization's purpose can

provide a stable anchor for team members, helping them stay focused and resilient.

- **Attracts and Retains Talent.** Organizations known for a clear and compelling purpose are more attractive to potential employees and have a better chance of retaining top talent who seek more than just a paycheck.
- **Aligns Individual Aspirations with Business Goals.** By connecting employees to the organization's purpose, leaders can align individual aspirations with business goals, creating a harmonious work environment where personal and organizational objectives support each other.

Again, it comes down to individualizing the work experience. Here are two examples from the same company but internalized differently by two leaders.

A leader named Cindy told me she loved marketing for a healthcare technology company. She knew the organization was changing lives by designing new technologies for people to improve their mobility. Her mother was wheelchair-bound, so she knew how difficult it could be when mobility becomes a challenge. Cindy felt a deep sense of pride when she told people where she worked because she believed her company's purpose aligns with her purpose.

Her colleague Jerry worked for the same company. He was in sales and believed in the products he sold. Having worked for a healthcare technology company that was not very ethical, he prided himself on the high ethical standards that the company lived out. Trust and ethics are the cornerstones of his values and having the opportunity to work for such a purpose-driven company helped him live out *his* purpose in life.

Two very different stories from two successful people, yet they both have passion for their organizations because what is essential to their purpose in life aligned with the organization.

As a leader, how do you ensure your team members feel that their purpose and mission align with the organization? By having a dialogue about what is essential to each person, you can help guide them in focusing on the areas where the organization aligns with their purpose.

Through building these trusting relationships and individualizing the employee experience, along with the understanding, communication, and culture work discussed in earlier chapters, leaders succeed by making purposeful connections between individuals and organizations.

Here are a few examples that are similar to connecting through place, but focused on purpose to engage your team members:

- **Storytelling.** Share examples of how the organization lives out its vision, mission, and values. Find opportunities to share stories of how customers' lives have been improved due to the organization's work.
- **Rewards and Recognition.** Reward and recognize team members who exemplify organizational values.
- **Volunteerism.** Find local community causes to support that align with the organizational purpose and provide employees time off to volunteer.
- **Conversations.** Ask team members how they think their values and purpose align with the company values and purpose. Provide opportunities for group discussions and reflection.

Connecting yourself and your team members to your organization's purpose is beneficial—actually, it's essential to fostering a productive, innovative, and committed workforce.

We know the benefits for people and organizations when we create workplaces designed to engage our team members. By using the Leaders SUCCEED together© system and focusing on 1. Place, 2. People, and 3. Purpose, you will create an engaged workforce.

Chapter Summary

Leaders own the employee experience and are responsible for employee engagement, which is the spark that can drive results to the next level and retain top talent.

- **Leader Engagement.** Engaged leaders are better prepared to lead others. Those leaders who recognize that their emotions and attitudes are contagious set the tone for their teams.
- **Emotional Engagement.** A key focus is on the broader definition of employee engagement, which encompasses the emotional and psychological commitment to work and organizational goals. Since it's impossible for team members to operate as two different selves, personal and professional, leaders who succeed strive to engage each person's entire self.
- **Benefits of Engagement.** The benefits of employee engagement are clear, like increased productivity, improved retention, enhanced well-being, higher customer satisfaction, innovation, effective change management, positive organizational culture, and financial impact.
- **Three Components of Expectations in the Leaders SUCCEED together© System.** Leaders foster engagement through supportive environments, growth opportunities, meaningful work, and open communication created by focusing on three areas of engagement within the Leaders SUCCEED together© system, 1. Place 2. People, and 3. Purpose, each playing a unique role in enhancing engagement.
    1. **Place.** We all naturally attach to physical and virtual spaces. Leaders who create belonging and connection to the workplace can leverage the value of the global workforce and retain the most talented team members.

2. **People.** Relationships at work matter and intentionally connecting people to the customers they serve and one another is worth the time and effort.
3. **Purpose.** Leaders who define their own purpose and connect it with the organizational purpose will become more engaged. Focus on aligning team members with the organization's purpose for enhanced engagement. This involves storytelling, rewards and recognition, alignment with company values, volunteerism, and meaningful conversations about personal and organizational purposes.

Focusing on place, people, and purpose creates a highly engaged workforce, which can be a competitive advantage for organizations. Using the Leaders SUCCEED together© system, leaders can significantly impact employee engagement and organizational success by igniting the spark that resides in each of us—the spark of engagement.

Now, let's Do, Reflect, and Discuss to apply what we have learned about engagement.

Do

1. Locate engagement surveys you have within your organization and read the information. If you don't have any surveys, review the latest State of the Workforce report from Gallup.
2. Make note of your surroundings at work. Make a list of how you are or are not connected from a place, people, and purpose perspective.
3. Make a list of the team members you have and use three columns (Place, People, Purpose) to check where your team members are or are not demonstrating engagement.

Reflect

1. Think about your level of engagement. What might you do to increase your connections to place, people, and purpose at work?
2. Review the list you made of your team members. What actions could you take to connect your team members more deeply to place, people, and purpose?
3. Are there areas where you need to resolve issues from a workspace, conflict, or purpose-alignment perspective for yourself or others at work?

Discuss

1. What is your organization doing well, and where might you improve on engaging team members by leveraging their place at work?
2. What is your organization doing well, and where might you improve on engaging team members by deepening connections between people at work?
3. Where might you improve engagement by connecting team members to the organization's purpose?

Chapter 8: Development

The Leadership Growth Engine

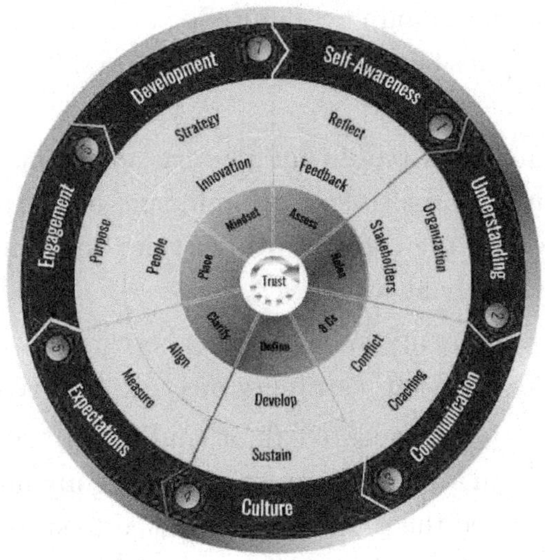

And now we are at the final step in the Leaders SUCCEED together© system. You might be wondering what keeps the engine of this system going. The answer? The last step: Development.

The only way we as leaders continually move forward and get better every day and every year is if we commit to developing ourselves and those around us.

Foundation for Development

If someone asked me how my career began with such a quick start, I would tell them that it was due to my coop experience and management training program. Unfortunately, many organizations have shifted away from this practice. I urge them to reconsider investing in these early work experiences and training programs for team members because they pay significant dividends for our future workforce.

In college I was an intern at a local phone company in the marketing department. My boss was an artist who hated spreadsheets, and I loved them. It was a perfect match. Like I shared in the beginning, math didn't compute for me, but spreadsheets did. In fact, my colleagues bought me a sign that says, "Ooh, this calls for a spreadsheet!"

My internship boss taught me the art side of marketing, and I supported her in data. I also learned mundane-but-important things like how not to jam the copier, how to write an email, and how to interact professionally at work.

One day I was in my cubicle, and she came in and said, "Go upstairs and take notes for a strategy meeting they're having."

I knew that was the executive floor, and I was thrilled. I grabbed my notepad and ran for the elevator, smoothing my business suit on the way up. I entered the room and was asked to sit in the back and take the notes. As I sat there, I recorded the meeting notes and considered the conversation.

This was the late 80's, when a payphone was still on every corner. The company was raking in tons of cash from these, while seeing some growth in pagers. The leaders, who had all been with the company for over 20 years, were discussing if they should support cell phones as a product. At this time, these were bag phones you carried around or car phones.

The conversation went like this: "These cell phones have no future. They're too big! And no one needs them because there's a pay phone on every corner and pagers that let you call people back."

Sitting there in my early twenties, I was thinking about how great it would be to have a cell phone. But, clearly, I was in the minority. The meeting ended with everyone believing that cell phones had no future.

Over time I watched as that company fell further and further behind in the cell phone market. I promised myself that I would never discount innovation like that, and that I would always ask the least tenured person in the room what they thought. It was the development experience of a lifetime!

When I graduated from college, I entered a management training program at a bank. It was rotational, so I learned more in a year than I could have ever imagined. The leader I was assigned to was the youngest female VP in the company, and she was my idol. Smart, poised, and scary to many people. She didn't take anything from anyone. Although I can name at least twenty leaders who positively influenced me over my career, she was the most impactful. Under her leadership I built *my* leadership foundation.

She developed me by giving me amazing opportunities to lead and work on projects and was kind enough later to help me find a role in Cleveland when I met the love of my life.

Working with a strong leader who was also a mentor allowed me to grow in ways I never could have if the only option were to take on a standard role within the organization. The leadership programs I attended at various stages in my career, my MBA, and my Ph.D. work all contributed to the learnings reflected in this system.

One of the most challenging situations is when I work with people who have been in the work world for years, and they missed out on this development. A man who is 65 told me that he has learned more about leadership in the eight-month program I did for his organization than he had in his entire career. I should have been happy, but it made me very sad. To think that he had missed out on so much because no one invested in his development.

Another 40-year-old woman reached out to me. She said that she didn't think she could be a leader because she worked remotely and was a project manager who never received any leadership development. My message to these people is that it is never too late to develop yourself, and the message to organizations is to focus efforts on designing ways to develop leaders at every level to create better organizations for all of us.

Continuously developing means stretching ourselves outside of work. Because I've got news for you—work is only *part* of our lives. At one point in my career, I thought I had arrived. But then I realized that my journey had only just begun.

Personal Growth Leads to Professional

After achieving success at the global bank, I volunteered with local children's homes and won the president's award for volunteerism. I didn't know that award existed until I received a certificate in the mail! I thought I was doing well—serving on local boards and raising two young children with my husband, who had an equally-demanding job.

Then one day the children's home said they had a 15-year-old girl they wanted me to mentor. I accepted the role, doing what I could to reunite her with her mother. Unfortunately, reunification didn't work, and she needed a family.

My husband and I both had busy careers, and honestly had no idea what to do with a teen. But we are people of faith, and we prayed about the situation. We both felt called to bring her into our home as our daughter.

Anyone who has ever adopted a child or blended a family will tell you that during the process they learned a lot about themselves and how to navigate uncertain waters. It all worked out, and our family of four became a family of five with more love to go around. During this time and even to this day, I am thankful for how this personal experience helped me grow as a human and leader. Making mistakes, doing your best, and accepting things you can't control are all lessons I needed to embrace personally and professionally.

Think about the challenges in your life and never underestimate the amount of growth that can happen outside of work that will bring a new perspective to what you do to make a living. Stretching ourselves beyond what is comfortable can take us to places we never dreamed possible.

This is why the final focus area in the Leaders SUCCEED together© system is for leaders to invest in developing mindsets, increasing innovation, and crafting strategies that will become an ongoing process for becoming the leaders they were meant to be.

Intentional Development Design

Designing development opportunities in an organization involves creating a culture and structure that supports continuous growth, learning, and improvement at every level. Sometimes, given all the responsibilities, leaders struggle to prioritize development for themselves and their teams. Organizations collectively spend over 61 billion dollars per year on leadership development.[37]

A recent Harvard Business Review article cites consistent areas needed for success: focus on the whole person, opportunities for self-reflection, and target programs that reduce stress and address psychological barriers to growth. Their research also found both short intensive programs and online programs can be just as effective as longer in-person programs.[38]

A recent quote from research at McKinsey states, "Investing in workers is good for organizations, too—to the tune of $1 billion in economic profit for those that focus on both performance and people."[39] The report explains that organizations limit themselves when they only hire people with certain degrees and overlook those they may be able to develop.

The three areas to focus on during the final step of the Leaders SUCCEED together© system are: 1. Mindset, 2. Innovation, and 3. Strategy.

1. Mindset

If there is one barrier to success for leaders outside of a lack of self-awareness, it would be their mindset. What we say to ourselves determines our feelings and actions and directly impacts our work.

I went to a craft fair with my daughter, and at one of the booths, they were selling shirts that read, "What you say to yourself matters. BE NICE!"

That message is straightforward, but to reinforce it even further, I often ask clients who berate themselves, "What would you say to a friend who made the same mistake?"

They pause and look at me for a moment when they realize they would never say the things they are thinking about themselves to a friend. What goes on in our brains influences our feelings and actions, so learning how to control our mindsets can mean the difference between success and failure for leaders. This is why removing barriers and broadening and embracing a growth mindset are all part of developing into the leaders we were meant to be.

Removing Barriers

The tapes that play in our minds that construct our reality about what we can accomplish have profound and tangible consequences. Throughout my life, I have struggled with depression in various seasons. During a time I was in therapy and doing research on the topic, I found a process I applied to myself and share with many clients to improve the way they think.

One point I must make here: Most coaches, like me, are not licensed therapists, and it's unethical for us to present ourselves as such. If clients are struggling with mental health issues, I always recommend they seek a therapist. My expertise lies in business and leadership coaching, not therapy. I never cross that line.

However, I will share resources across business and psychology whenever I find them helpful. For example, there's a book by Dr. David Burns called *Feeling Good*, where he shares common cognitive distortions.[40] From a coaching perspective, I also include cognitive biases that often limit how many leaders think.

Here are eleven examples of cognitive biases and distortions that Dr. David Burns has identified that could be impacting your mindset:

1. **All-or-Nothing Thinking.** You see things as black or white. If your performance falls short, you are a total failure.
2. **Overgeneralization.** You see one negative event as a never-ending pattern of defeat.
3. **Mental Filter.** You pick out one negative event and dwell on it exclusively so that your vision of reality is darkened by one situation.
4. **Disqualifying the Positive.** You reject positive experiences and believe they don't count in order to hold on to a negative belief.
5. **Jumping to Conclusions.** You make a negative interpretation even though there are no definite facts to support it. This is also mind-reading, where you arbitrarily conclude someone is reacting negatively to you and you don't bother to check it out.
6. **Fortune Telling.** You are convinced that things will turn out badly and assume it is already a fact.

7. **Catastrophizing or Minimization.** You exaggerate your own mistakes or shortcomings and minimize those of others or your own achievements.
8. **Emotional Reasoning.** You assume that your negative emotions reflect reality. I feel it, therefore, it is. Feelings lie a lot, so beware.
9. **Should Statements.** You try to motivate yourself with should statements to make yourself feel guilty. 'Musts' or 'oughts' are also culprits. Don't 'should' on yourself!
10. **Labeling and Mislabeling.** Making statements like, "I'm a loser," or, "I'm so stupid." Also, you may find yourself mislabeling an event in a highly emotional way, thinking it was a total disaster. Was it really?
11. **Personalization.** You see yourself as the cause of some negative external event when you weren't responsible for it. For example: "It was all my fault." Really, was it?

To combat these barriers within our minds, I offer a simple three-step model that many of my clients have used to overcome these ways of thinking and change their mindset: 1. Name it, 2. Frame it, and 3. Reframe it. At the core, it's about questioning our thinking to change and, in many cases, cleaning up what we say to ourselves.

Clean Up Your Mindset

I had a client who thought she did a terrible job on a presentation, and she called me in a panic. "It was a total disaster," she said. "I'm going to get fired!"

After hearing her talk about the situation, we worked through the process. I asked if anything good had happened. She said yes, the potential client seemed to like her, and they had good questions. I asked about the evidence she had that she was going to be fired. She couldn't think of any except that she was assuming her boss would be angry that she didn't get the account signed at the meeting.

We took out the list of cognitive distortions, and I asked her to name it, meaning that she was likely experiencing a mindset influenced by some biases. Then I asked her to frame it, acknowledging biases that might be influencing her mindset. She was able to name about four of them: catastrophizing, fortune telling, jumping to conclusions, discounting the positive, and framing the situation as being influenced by how she was thinking at the time when she was very stressed.

Finally, I then asked her to try to reframe it and describe the situation again without these biases impacting her mindset. She said, "I had a rough presentation today and may not get the account. Next time, I will anticipate more questions and be better prepared." She then reinforced the growth mindset we had been working on by saying the experience provided a good learning opportunity for her.

The name it, frame it, and reframe it process takes practice, but it is often one of the most impactful workshops I teach for professionals, because it connects to emotional intelligence in managing our emotions and controlling the thoughts that go through our minds.

The psychological triangle connecting our thoughts, feelings, and actions, and the order in which they occur has been debated for centuries. I know that whatever is in our minds impacts our feelings and actions, and they are all related. So, if we can develop stronger mindsets, we are more likely to succeed at becoming the leaders we were meant to be.

A side note about the client who thought she would be fired: She learned the potential client was distracted by a challenge at work that day, but later ended up signing a contract based on her presentation. So instead of getting fired, she got a raise. And think of the wasted time she spent in her mind!

Broaden Your View

Another aspect of mindset I work with leaders on is to shift how they view themselves and their role within the organization. We all know that organizations have an inverse cone-shaped structure, so the higher you go as you are promoted, the fewer opportunities are available. We will all hit the side wall of the cone at some point unless we become the CEO. However, many people hit that wall (or ceiling) much earlier because they maintain a narrow mindset.

Rethinking Your Mindset

When you take on a leadership role for the first time, you can rethink how you view your role. For example, I was working with a client who was frustrated that he kept getting passed over for promotions. He had been promoted to division leader and remained there for almost ten years. But after a few conversations, it was clear why this was happening.

He didn't realize that he had not broadened his thinking past this role to include the entire organization. His communication was always about his division and his team. Although he was promoted, he had not broadened his mindset to include the entire organization. I see that not thinking like a CEO is a core limiter for people in organizations who find themselves stuck in middle leadership roles.

So, how do you broaden your mindset? Here are a few practical ways:

- **Sit in the Seat Exercise.** When you think about organizational situations, pretend that you're sitting in the CEO's seat and consider alternatives from that perspective. Instead of looking at decisions you make from only your role, sit in the seat of the CEO and see how your perspective may change. Through this exercise, you will find that you may have to make tradeoffs that don't always put your department's needs above others, or that you must give up resources for the overall good of the organization. Leaders who demonstrate that they think more like the organization's CEO will be viewed as strategic leaders.

- **Communication.** Analyze how you are communicating. What do you see when you review emails and conversations with people internally and external to the organization? Are you sharing information in ways that demonstrate your interest in the entire organization, or are you only considering your team and role? Are you using terms and behaving in ways that align with the strategy and values of the organization? The subtle queues we make as we communicate daily will establish how others view us.
- **Staying Updated.** Although not every CEO stays up to date on the latest technology and market trends, the best ones do, and they read a lot. Take time to read and keep updated so that you can constantly broaden your mindset. Read the Wall Street Journal, Harvard Business Review, MIT Sloan, and other articles related to your specific industry and business. Staying updated on trends, like what is happening now with artificial intelligence and other technologies, will allow you to expand your perspective and keep a broadened mindset.

Embrace a Growth Mindset

Along with removing barriers and broadening your mindset, developing a growth mindset is critical for leaders. The concepts of growth and fixed mindsets, initially developed by psychologist Carol Dweck, provide a framework for understanding how individuals perceive their abilities and intelligence and how this perception impacts their learning, effort, and resilience. [41]

A growth mindset is one where you believe your abilities and intelligence can be developed through dedication, hard work, and persistence. If you approach challenges with a growth mindset, you will embrace them as opportunities to grow and learn, persist even with setbacks, and even if you fail, you will see it as part of learning and not a reflection of your abilities.

In contrast, people with a fixed mindset believe that intelligence and abilities are static traits that can't be developed because they are inherent and unchangeable. When faced with challenges, people with a fixed mindset tend to avoid them and give up in the face of failure, or they view it as a direct measure of their ability or intelligence. Those with growth mindsets are also more likely to support the success of others and embrace constructive criticism, versus those with fixed mindsets, who can be easily offended and jealous when others succeed.

As a leader, when we develop a growth mindset for ourselves and guide our team members toward the same, we will be more likely to succeed together.

Once you have removed barriers, broadened, and set your mindset toward growth, the next two areas for leaders to ensure development within the Leaders SUCCEED together© system is to develop innovation and strategy to succeed.

2. Innovation

Leading innovation from any position within an organization, regardless of rank or title, involves cultivating a culture of creativity and forward-thinking. While working with an organization on improving their customer experience, one CEO said he was incredibly frustrated that his team would not come up with any innovative ideas. As I observed a few meetings, I went to him and said that I thought I knew the problem and asked if he wanted to hear it. Sometimes, people don't want your advice, even if they pay you for it, so I needed to know if he was ready for some hard truths.

I explained that in each meeting I observed, his team members deferred to him for every decision because of the way he was communicating. When someone raised an idea, the rest of the group would look at him to see how he responded before they would add to it, agree, or disagree. Over time, he unintentionally created a culture where his team could leave their brains at home because he was expected to do all the thinking.

We know that innovation can happen anywhere in organizations, but it must have space to develop and grow. Instead of responding and making decisions like the group expected, I encouraged him to ask questions and encourage dialogue to generate more ideas.

Another organization I worked within was not innovative, and I became very frustrated because I love to innovate. After working there for a while, I found out that there was an invisible penalty box for anyone who tried something and failed, so no one wanted to experiment or suggest new ideas. This lack of innovation put the organization behind competitors.

With the change that is occurring all around us, we know organizations need to innovate to survive. Here are a few practical ways you can develop and support innovation as a leader:

- **Foster Open Communication & Collaboration.** Create an environment where ideas can be freely shared and discussed without judgment. Open lines of communication encourage collaborative thinking and the cross-pollination of ideas. Leverage technology and discovering ways to share information that leads to people being able to build upon the ideas of others and easily collaborate.
- **Empower Team Members.** Give employees the autonomy and authority to explore new ideas and approaches. Empowerment

can boost confidence to encourage innovative thinking and embrace diverse perspectives. Leverage the strengths of individuals and give them room to make mistakes, learn, and grow.

- **Lead by Example.** Model innovative thinking and risk-taking. Show that you value creativity and are willing to explore new approaches and ideas. Share the information you have learned and ask how people think this might be leveraged within your organization. Be curious and open to ideas by allowing people to learn and explore, even if it means they may fail. Share some of your own failures so your team knows that it's OK to try and fail.
- **Recognize and Reward Innovation**. Acknowledge and reward creative ideas and innovations. Recognition can be a powerful motivator for continued innovation. Celebrate successes and invite people to be open about initiatives they have tried that have not worked to send a clear message that you will support people who try new things and fail, as long as they learn and are open to continuously improving.
- **Challenge the Status Quo.** Regularly question existing processes and practices and encourage your team to do the same. Ask, "What if?" and "Why not?" to stimulate thinking beyond current constraints. Make it a common practice to use design thinking or agile methodologies to shift mindsets and embrace new ideas.

As you spend time developing your mindset and ability to lead innovation, the final area of development that differentiates leaders is how they approach strategy within their organizations for professional development, their teams, and their professional growth.

3. Strategy

When I facilitate professional development programs, many leaders find that they don't have strengths specific to strategic thinking, so they assume that they can rely on someone else for strategy. Unfortunately, that does not work well because every leader within the organization needs to understand how their role contributes to the organization's overall strategic direction and be proactive in how they lead in this area.

The good news is that you don't have to be a strategist to be strategic. Still, you do need to force yourself to craft and align strategy, or you will find that many of the other areas of this book we discussed will not come together.

One of the main reasons I'm called into executive coaching engagements is that the leader is not strategic and frustrating the C-level executive. It's usually not that they are unwilling to be more strategic, but that being more tactical and focused on the details is where they are comfortable. That has led to success in the past, so they don't have a strong desire to shift out of their comfort zone and learn strategy. However, if you want to differentiate yourself as a leader, developing a great strategy is the place to do it.

Here are a few ways to lead strategy from anywhere within an organization:

- **Understand the Big Picture.** Gain a thorough understanding of the organization's mission, vision, values, goals, and challenges. This knowledge provides a foundation for strategic thinking. It builds upon what we discussed in the previous section on developing a growth mindset and staying informed with industry knowledge and trends. Connecting your work to the organizational mission, vision, and values and knowing how you contribute to the strategic plan will set a strong foundation for leading strategy.

- **Develop Strong Analytical Skills.** Hone your ability to analyze data, interpret metrics, and understand financial reports. This skillset is essential for making informed strategic decisions. Many clients tell me they aren't great at math, so they rely on a business analyst or CFO to be responsible for the financial numbers.
  However, leaders who know the numbers will be viewed as more credible. Push yourself to understand how the numbers work together within your organization, where profit and losses are coming from, and what levers may need to be shifted to improve in various areas. Remember, I almost failed algebra, but somehow, I figured out structural equation modeling in my Ph.D. program because I relentlessly focused on developing my analytical skills. If I can do it, anyone can!
- **Cultivate a Network of Relationships.** Build relationships across different levels and departments. A diverse network can provide insights and support the implementation of strategic initiatives to work collaboratively with others to develop solutions to complex challenges. Collaboration can lead to more comprehensive and robust strategies. Take the initiative to identify issues and propose solutions. Don't wait for instructions; demonstrate your ability to lead strategically by being proactive.
- **Actively Participate in Strategic Discussions.** Actively engage in strategic meetings and discussions, even if you're not in a senior position. Offer insights and suggestions that demonstrate your strategic thinking. Regularly seek feedback on your ideas and be open to suggestions from others. Feedback can provide new insights and help refine your strategic approaches. Ensure that your strategic ideas and initiatives align with the overall goals and objectives of the organization. This alignment is crucial for the successful implementation of any strategy.

By cultivating these skills and approaches, leaders at any level can effectively contribute to strategy development and demonstrate their strategic acumen, enhancing their influence and impact within the organization.

The next area for strategic development is creating a professional development strategy for your team.

Professional Development Strategy for Your Team

Sometimes within organizations I find talent hoarders. Those leaders who believe they need to hold on to anyone with talent within their organization and not let them leave their group. I'm not talking about working to retain great people within your organization. I'm talking about holding people back from roles that would allow them to grow.

As I look back on my career, my proudest moments have been when I have worked to develop a leader and then see them go on to do great things outside of my area. To be known as someone who can develop talent is a reputation we should all be proud to cultivate.

Think back to the leaders who have helped develop you. Or, sadly, maybe you haven't experienced one yet and have been out here all alone, for which I'm sorry.

Here are a few ways to create a strategy for professional development for your team members:

- **Customize Development to the Individual.** Understand each employee's unique needs and goals and tailor development plans accordingly. The nature of this book requires your leadership development program to be somewhat standard. However, please don't misuse or misinterpret this resource. Yes, I believe everyone can benefit from the key learnings of this book. However, not everyone should have the same development program. Leaders should develop with leaders in similar positions and roles, or you stifle growth. Executives want to learn with other executives and frontline managers want to be comfortable learning with their peers. This is why I offer a variety of programs that are specific to certain stages of leadership and individualized coaching. As leaders, we can help others succeed by tailoring development to their specific needs.

- **Combine the Power of Coaching and Mentoring**. Since we discussed coaching in the earlier chapter, now is a great time to introduce it again, but in a different context. The value of investing in qualified professional coaching is backed by research, with some citing a 788% return on investment.[42] However, some organizations are trying to save money or believe that they can coach using internal coaches. I am strongly opposed to this method, which has nothing to do with having my consulting and coaching practice.

  Even before I began executive coaching, I saw how internal coaching could be limiting. It seems like it would be more cost-effective to hire a team of internal coaches. However, there are a myriad of issues with this approach. The clients I've had who participated in these programs have shared that they were not effective because they didn't believe their conversations could be kept confidential. Something less expensive isn't always more effective.

  Mentoring, however, by internal leaders can be highly effective. Mentoring is different from coaching. Mentors share expertise and experience. It's a transfer of knowledge between one person to the other. Establish a feedback mechanism that includes input from peers, subordinates, and supervisors to provide a comprehensive view of an employee's performance and development areas.
- **Offer Cross-Functional Experiences & Skill Development.** Early in my career, a boss of mine told me that A players hire A

players because they want the best talent on their teams, and B players hire C players because they are afraid talented people will outshine them. This quote has stuck with me, along with others. Like, "If you find yourself the smartest person in the room, find another room."

As leaders we should always look to hiring people who are better than we are. As evidenced in this book, I care deeply about leveraging each person's talent. I also know that for people to stretch themselves, they need to gain cross-functional experience. When I hear stories from clients about how their leader will not allow them to take on a stretch role within the company because they don't want to lose them, I become concerned.

We all want to retain talented employees, but talent hoarders do not help people and organizations grow. This is why successful leaders focus on developing their teams and seek opportunities for team members to expand their skills. If I had never had a leader push me to take on a sales role, I would have remained in operations and never developed the critical skills I use to this day. Sure, she lost me out of operations, but I was able to help grow an entire division by joining sales and, with the operational mindset I had, was able to mend some bridges between the areas.

- **Ensure the Program Is Research-Based.** Invest in career development, leadership, and training initiatives based on solid research to nurture future leaders within the organization. Often, I find leadership development programs created by well-meaning and talented professionals that are outdated or missing vital information about what we know about human behavior. Sadly, this occurs because most don't want to spend significant time updating materials and checking to validate the theories underpinning what is being shared.

I remember attending a leadership seminar not too long ago, where the sandwich approach was taught as an appropriate method to share feedback. Leadership theory and practice have evolved far from this method. As I sat there listening, I was disappointed that these young professionals were not receiving proper guidance based on what we know today.

Our most valuable asset is our leaders. Locating up-to-date and research-based resources is worth the effort. Our teams will enhance their leadership skills, emotional intelligence, and strategic thinking by providing strong leadership development through workshops, coaching, and mentoring integrated within these types of programs.

- **Set Clear Goals and Measures for Success**. One challenge many organizations have is how to measure success. Since leadership development involves people and varying contexts, it isn't easy to measure effectiveness directly. However, you can still look at the number of people promoted, retention rates, and other metrics to measure success.
- **Provide Career Pathing and Planning.** Whatever method you use for talent planning (e.g., 9-box, calibration, etc.), ensure you have a process to determine the bench strength within the organization. Middle managers are at the heart of your organization, so don't forget to focus on their development. Especially the younger generations entering the workforce—they want to know they are contributing and growing.

  That doesn't mean they need to see a path from their role to the CEO. It does mean that they need to feel valued and feel they can progress. A student in one of my MBA courses told me that everyone focused on development in the military because you aren't allowed to move from your position until you have a trained backfill. That's a solid motivation to always develop a bench of people who could take on your role. Every organization could benefit from leaders who focus on career pathing and planning.

Professional Development Strategy for Yourself

As we are in the home stretch of this book, you will see that you have discovered some insights about yourself. By now you probably know where you need to focus and what you want to put into action.

Here are the next steps for you to craft a development strategy to become the leader you were meant to be:

1. **Create a Vision.** To start, leaders who succeed define a clear and inspiring vision for their own professional development. This vision encompasses their long-term career goals, the skills they want to acquire, and the impact they aspire to make. Vision sets the direction and purpose for the entire development plan.
2. **Develop a Plan.** After establishing a vision, successful leaders create a structured and detailed development plan. This plan outlines specific goals, milestones, and strategies to achieve their vision. It also includes actionable steps, timelines, and resources required to make progress effectively.
3. **Enlist the Right Support.** Successful leaders recognize that they can't achieve their development goals in isolation. They work to enlist the support of mentors, coaches, peers, or colleagues who can provide guidance, feedback, and expertise. Building a solid support network is crucial for gaining valuable insights and overcoming challenges.
4. **Track Progress.** Influential leaders regularly monitor and evaluate their progress. They establish key performance indicators (KPIs) or benchmarks to assess their progress toward their development goals. Tracking progress allows for adjustments, identifies improvement areas, and ensures alignment with the overall plan.

5. **Celebrate Success or Redirect.** When leaders reach significant milestones or achieve their development goals, it's important to celebrate their successes. Recognizing and celebrating achievements provides motivation and a sense of accomplishment. However, if progress stalls or goals change, successful leaders are open to redirection and willing to adapt their plan accordingly.

And here we are, at the seventh step of the Leaders SUCCEED together© system for growth. Although this is the final step of the system, think of development as not a conclusion, but a lifelong commitment to growth. Seeking development keeps you agile, innovative, and strategic, ensuring that you and your team are constantly evolving.

In a world that never stops changing, your commitment to development is what will move you forward to becoming the vision of the leader you were meant to be.

Chapter Summary

In this finale of the Leaders SUCCEED together© system, development, I challenge you to commit yourself to the growth journey that may take a lifetime to complete. Are you up for it?

Within the final step of development, the three focus areas that will take leaders to the next level and help them succeed are 1. Mindset 2. Innovation, and 3. Strategy.

1. **Mindset: The Powerhouse of Leadership.**
   - **Conquering Cognitive Distortions.** Mindset in leadership can be an enabler or derailer. Identifying and overcoming cognitive distortions and biases is key. Leaders can transform negative self-talk into a positive, growth-oriented mindset by using strategies like naming, framing, and reframing thoughts.

- **Broadening Perspectives.** The ability to think beyond immediate roles and envision broader organizational impacts is highlighted. This includes exercises like the 'sit in the CEO's seat,' and encouraging leaders to adopt a strategic, big-picture view.
- **Developing a Growth Mindset.** Leaders who succeed understand that fixed mindsets limit success, so they create mindsets focused on growth for themselves and coach those on their teams to see failures as opportunities for growth, not obstacles to their success.

2. **Innovation: Cultivating a Culture of Creativity**
   - **Encouraging Open Communication & Collaboration.** Leaders can foster environments where ideas die or flourish. This involves empowering teams, leading by example, rewarding innovation, and challenging the status quo.
   - **Overcoming Barriers to Innovation.** Real-world examples illustrate how innovation can be stifled by leadership styles and how to overcome these challenges.
3. **Strategy: Crafting the Future**
   - **Strategic Thinking for Every Leader.** The importance of strategic thinking at all levels is underscored. Leaders understand the big picture, develop strong analytical skills, cultivate networks, and actively engage in strategic discussions.
   - **Professional Development: Dual Paths for Growth**
     - **For Your Team.** Tailoring development to individual team members is crucial. Combine coaching and mentoring, offering cross-functional experiences, and ensuring research-based programs are highlighted as key strategies. It's important to not just retain talent, but to nurture, encourage, and grow it.

  - **For Yourself.** Leaders are urged to create their own vision and development plan, enlist support, track progress, and be open to redirection. This personal development journey is marked by setting clear goals and celebrating milestones, underlining the need for continuous learning and adaptation.
- **The Ongoing Journey of Development.** Development in leadership isn't an endpoint, but a perpetual cycle of growth and improvement. Leaders who view development as an integral, unending component of their leadership journey will bring out the best in themselves and those around them.

The Leaders SUCCEED together© system is a roadmap for lifelong learning, innovation, and strategic thinking. I hope you have discovered that true leadership development is an ever-evolving process, one that requires dedication, self-awareness, and an unwavering commitment to growth. As you step forward, carry the torch of development, illuminating your path to becoming the leader you were meant to be and inspiring others to join you on this remarkable journey.

Now, let's Do, Reflect, and Discuss this final step of development within the Leaders SUCCEED together© system.

Do

1. Practice the naming, framing, and reframing technique at least three times.
2. Identify potential ways your organization could innovate and assess how you are currently handling innovation.
3. Create an outline for a strategic plan for your area based on the goals you need to achieve.

Reflect

1. Reading through the biases and cognitive distortions, is there one that you typically struggle with?
2. If there were no constraints, what would you do to innovate within your organization?
3. How can you create a strategy for yourself to develop that aligns with the organizational strategy?

Discuss

1. Share an example where your mindset got in the way of a change you were working to implement.
2. Talk about how you are going to influence your organization to be more innovative.
3. Discuss your personal and professional strategic goals.

Chapter 9: What's Next?

Now that you have learned the Leaders SUCCEED together© system, you may have discovered leadership areas where you are strong and have also identified skills you would like to continue to develop.

The leadership journey never ends. As this book began, we agreed that we are all leaders because we influence those around us. As such, we have a responsibility to ourselves and others to continue to invest in the lives of other people.

I'm sure you can name some people who have positively impacted you in your life, even though they may not have seen themselves as a leader. When we embrace the Leaders SUCCEED together© system, we recognize that Leaders SUCCEED together in the community by creating clarity about their vision for the future and their goals and by maintaining strong connections.

Here is what I recommend as the next steps to bring it all together to become the leader you were meant to be: 1. Community, 2. Clarity, and 3. Connection.

1. Community

During my doctoral studies I leaned heavily on a group we decided to call the Ph.D. Sisterhood. There were five of us out of 20 in the cohort who were women, so we bonded together with a commitment that no matter what we would graduate. Little did I know the lifeline that group would be for me.

As I reentered an educational setting, the little girl from the beginning of this book reappeared. I doubted myself to the point that I had to be placed on medication and ended up in the hospital for over a week after a bad reaction.

These women sustained me during one of the most challenges times of my life. I was sitting in the car crying at one of my daughter's cheer practices, telling one of these sisterhood members how I couldn't continue getting my Ph.D. because I wasn't smart enough or good enough. Thankfully, she convinced me otherwise and told me how wrong I was.

Being in community with other leaders and people who are on the path toward success is what will take you from understanding the principles in this book to levering them to achieve your own success.

Recently, I was leading a group-coaching session for leaders, and I asked what they had learned most from the program. One of the participants said that he was so relieved there wasn't just one leadership style, because he thought that he had to become someone he was not.

Another participant said something I have heard often in my sessions, and it's honestly part of what makes this work my purpose and passion. He said, "Through this program, and by talking to other leaders in these sessions, I have learned that I am not broken."

Whenever the words *I am not broken* are stated as a key learning, it reminds me why leaders succeed best together and in a community. It also reinforces why I'm called to do and love this work.

There is a quote attributed to many authors that says, "If you want to go fast, go alone, but if you want to go far, go together." This saying is the essence of the journey of leadership.

I used to believe that being a great leader meant I had to do everything on my own and be the shiniest star in the galaxy. What I have learned, however, is that it is only within the community of other leaders, being vulnerable, and developing ourselves together that we become the best versions of ourselves.

Here are some practical ways to join a leadership community to become your best self and inspire others to become the leaders they were meant to be:

- **Mastermind Groups.** Over the years I have facilitated and participated in mastermind groups for a variety of organizations. This investment has provided value for years to come.
  I define masterminds as a one-time or ongoing event where a group of leaders come together to learn about a particular topic, and then they typically break into small groups for interactive discussions. Internal mastermind groups, such as those within employee resource groups (ERGs), can be great places to find supportive and open conversations.
  I once led a Global Women's Network for an organization, and the learnings we shared and the connections we built by coming together around a specific topic once a month pushed many women further faster in their careers.
  From a consulting and coaching perspective, I have had an opportunity to facilitate mastermind groups virtually and in-person on topics throughout this book for various organizations. The relationships that are created while everyone learns together are the most exciting to me!
- **Group Coaching.** As part of most of the leadership development programs I facilitate, I recommend group coaching because of how it reinforces the key learnings in a small and intimate setting of 6-8 leaders.
  At one point in my career, a friend invited me to his executive peer group's monthly meeting. In essence, this was a group-coaching session where everyone brought up 1-2 challenges they were facing for discussion. Of course, there was an agreement of 100% confidentiality, so you felt safe talking about real issues.
  We also agreed to ask good questions rather than solving issues for one another, because we know from research that the best

answers for people come from within. These group-coaching programs can be offered by organizations as well.
Always include a trained facilitator in these sessions. If someone is not in charge of leading the group, the meetings either won't happen or the conversations in the meetings get derailed. Both of which are frustrating to group members.
The two most reported benefits of these sessions are: 1. They are a place where people are solely focused on their success, and 2. They demonstrate that every leader experiences similar issues in different contexts.

- **Professional Organizations.** Some professional organizations offer leadership development opportunities and the ability to build a community of people you can trust to learn with during facilitated learning sessions. I have facilitated sessions for a variety of these organizations, and it reinforces that leaders learn best together. If you are involved in a professional organization, seek out learning opportunities that strengthen connections.
- **Leaders Succeed Community.** We are building a community for leaders who are interested in using and applying the Leaders SUCCEED together© system. Check out our website for mastermind groups, group coaching, and other opportunities to build community with other leaders.
- **Create Your Own.** If you don't find a community where you feel you can be authentically you, create your own! Get a few friends or colleagues together and start a leadership book club, work through the Leaders SUCCEED together© system, or host group-coaching sessions. Just remember the two rules: 1. Confidentiality, and 2. Facilitator.

It's easy to think we can do everything on our own until we realize it's impossible to be successful alone. I had a conversation recently with a leader who is convinced that you can't be a good leader until you have raised teenagers, because you don't understand how to deal with difficult people until that point in your life.

I believe that you don't need to endure that level of challenge in life or even have children, as long as you decide to take control over your own leadership development and join a community of leaders.

If you are up to the leadership challenge, then you can handle it. Just don't go it alone.

2. Clarity

You have spent time in this book reading, doing, reflecting, and hopefully discussing with other leaders. The "what's next" is to create a system to continue to grow. There will be concepts and pieces of the Leaders SUCCEED together© system that you will want to revisit and work on throughout your career. Staying on a clear path will help you on your journey.

Here is a format recommendation. You can choose the cadence of reviewing it, depending on your work style—be it daily, monthly, quarterly, or yearly. I recommend monthly, but many people feel better about checking off things daily. Whatever works to keep you on track and clear about where you're headed.

Here are a few items to consider:

- Professional Goals: 3-5 things I want to accomplish in my career.
- Personal Goals: 3-5 things I want to accomplish in my personal life. This can be relational, spiritual, financial, or whatever else is meaningful to you.
- Learning Goals: 3-5 things I want to learn, books I want to read, or something I want to investigate.
- Health Goals: 3-5 things I want to do to stay healthy.
- Service Goals: 3-5 people or organizations I can do more to help and support (personal or professional).

- 7 Question Reflection for Clarity (weekly, monthly, yearly):
    1. What accomplishments am I most proud of?
    2. What went well?
    3. What did not go well?
    4. How will I improve or shift directions?
    5. What else do I need to learn or do to grow?
    6. Am I living out my purpose and passion? (YES/NO)
    7. Am I the leader I want to be? (YES/NO)

These are just a few areas to track and reflect upon to continue your journey to becoming the leader you were meant to be by staying clear on your goals.

3. Connection

Leadership can be lonely. Especially as you rise to the top of an organization or seek to start or run your own company. There are few people who understand exactly what you're dealing with—people with whom you can trust to share your innermost struggles. The mental health crisis is really a crisis. So much so that I've chosen to end this book on that poignant note.

With so many digital distractions, it's easy to isolate ourselves. It's also easy to become stressed to the point of developing unhealthy habits or damaging our health. Connect with people who can support you in this leadership journey. Those connections will benefit your professional and personal life.

Here are just a few connections to consider:

- **Coach.** I used to believe that coaching was for people who couldn't handle their own issues. I thought it was all nonsense until I was at a crossroads in my career, and I hired my first professional coach. Now, I couldn't live without having someone I can trust as a coach who can help me collaborate on solutions to move forward.

Acknowledgments

Thank you.

Two words that never capture the true essence of the impact people have had on my life and during the journey of creating this system and book.

My husband, Jason, has been my rock and biggest inspiration over the past twenty-nine years. His own journey as a leader is a testament to how caring about people and leadership are one-in-the-same.

My children, Hunter, Lexi, and Serena have grown into loving adults and sacrificed time with their mom to allow me to live out my purpose, and I am truly grateful to see them embracing their unique gifts and talents.

My parents (Diana and Anthony), son-in-law (Zack), siblings direct and by marriage (Sonia and Scott, Joni and Mike, Brian, Jeremy and Kiona), in-laws (Terry and Barb), and all their families have demonstrated what it means to always strive to be your best and stick together no matter what.

My grandson, Bennett, gives me hope for the future generation of leaders with big hearts and much to accomplish.

The friends, students, coworkers, clients, leaders, professors, team members, fellow Ph.D. cohort members and sisters, along with so many other people have added insights and experiences to my life and this book—I am forever grateful.

Naming each person would fill too many pages, and I would be heartbroken to forget someone, so just know you are part of this story.

And thank you for taking your valuable time to invest in yourself. May you be the leader you were meant to be and take what you have learned to impact the lives of other people.

I believe that people enter your life for a reason, and that God is the one who is orchestrating these relationships and learnings, so I thank God for his ongoing blessings and guidance.

Eight years ago, I was sitting in church when the first seeds of this book were planted. I wrote as much as I could on the back of the church program that day. Every day since during my prayer time a question has been posed to me that has continued even through seasons of doubt: "Wouldn't the time and effort of writing this book be worth it if it helped change the life of just one person?"

My answer is finally *yes*.

About the Author

In addition to being the creator of the Leaders SUCCEED together© system, Dr. Angela Crawford is the founder of Crawford Partners, a consulting firm that specializes in strategy, leadership development, organizational design, business transformation, coaching, and employee experience.

With over 20 years of experience in senior level roles and consulting with Fortune 500 companies, Dr. Crawford endeavors to foster growth within people and organizations to help leaders become their very best, and to inspire new leaders in the next generation. Learn more at: www.leaderssucceedtogether.com.

Beyond her professional achievements, Dr. Crawford is committed to community and family. She has served on non-profit boards, supports her church and other charities, which is important to her mission. As an angel investor, mentor, and founder of AdvisorEz, she also lives out her desire to see entrepreneurship thrive.

Dr. Crawford earned her BBA in Marketing and Management from the University of Cincinnati, followed by an MBA from Cleveland State University and a Ph.D. from Case Western Reserve University. Her research on igniting passion within employees is published in the *Journal of Service Research*, and she holds certifications in Coaching, Cultural Intelligence, Mindfulness, and Strengths.

Angela resides in Northern Kentucky with her husband (Jason) of 29 years, dogs (Maverick & Goose) and cat (Cowboy) and is proud to be the mother of three grown children (Hunter, Lexi and Serena), son-in-law (Zack) and Mimi to her grandson (Bennett).

For further information regarding the author please visit:

LinkedIn: https://www.linkedin.com/in/angelaccrawford/

Book website: leaderssucceedtogether.com

Consulting practice website: crawfordpartnersllc.com

Citations

[1]https://www.gallup.com/workplace/285674/improve-employee-engagement-workplace.aspx

[2] Goleman, D., Boyatzis, R., & McKee, A. (2002). Primal leadership: The hidden driver of great performance. Harvard Business Review, 80(11), 42-51.

[3] Diener, E., & Fujita, F. (1995). Resources, personal strivings, and subjective well-being: A nomothetic and idiographic approach. Journal of Personality and Social Psychology, 68(5), 926-935.

[4] Day, D. V., Fleenor, J. W., Atwater, L. E., Sturm, R. E., & McKee, R. A. (2014). Advances in leader and leadership development: A review of 25 years of research and theory. The Leadership Quarterly, 25(6), 63-82.

[5] Goleman, D., Boyatzis, R. E., & McKee, A. (2002). Primal leadership: Realizing the power of emotional intelligence. Harvard Business Press.

[6] Kaplan, R. E., & Kaiser, R. B. (2017). Developing versatile leaders who can drive strategic change. MIT Sloan Management Review, 58(4), 75-81.

[7] Hogan, R., Kaiser, R. B., & Hogan, J. (2014). Management derailment: Personality assessment and mitigation. Journal of Managerial Psychology, 29(3), 279-300.

[8] Zweig, D. (2018). Microsoft CEO Satya Nadella on empathy and self-awareness. The Wall Street Journal. Retrieved from https://www.wsj.com/articles/microsoft-ceo-satya-nadella-on-empathy-and-self-awareness-1520343601

[9] Fernández-Aráoz, C., Roscoe, A., & Aramaki, K. (2017). Turning potential into success: The missing link in leadership development. Harvard Business Review, 95(5), 86-93

[10] Isaac, M., & Frenkel, S. (2017). Uber CEO Travis Kalanick resigns under investor pressure. The New York Times. Retrieved from https://www.nytimes.com/2017/06/21/technology/uber-ceo-travis-kalanick.html

[11] Goudreau, J. (2018). The real reason Uber became a toxic mess, according to a Stanford management professor. CNBC. Retrieved from https://www.cnbc.com/2018/02/06/the-real-reason-uber-became-a-toxic-mess-according-to-a-stanford-management-professor.html

[12] Goleman, Daniel. *Leadership: The power of emotional intelligence*. More Than Sound LLC, 2021.

[13] Giles, S. (2016, March 15). The Most Important Leadership Competencies, According to Leaders Around the World. Harvard Business Review. https://hbr.org/2016/03/the-most-important-leadership-competencies-according-to-leaders-around-the-world

[14] https://online.hbs.edu/blog/post/the-importance-of-reflective-leadership-in-business

[15]https://www.forbes.com/sites/tracybrower/2021/09/19/empathy-is-the-most-important-leadership-skill-according-to-research/?sh=77e92e4e3dc5

[16] Bass, B. M., & Riggio, R. E. (2006). Transformational leadership (2nd ed.). Psychology Press.

[17] Eisenbeiss, S. A., Knippenberg, D. V., & Boerner, S. (2008). Transformational leadership and team innovation: Integrating team climate principles. Journal of Applied Psychology, 93(6), 1438–1446.

[18]https://www.forbes.com/sites/forbescommunicationscouncil/2023/01/13/the-case-for-empathy-as-a-critical-skill-for-leaders/?sh=20f9453523b1

[19]https://www.forbes.com/sites/williamarruda/2023/02/15/why-most-new-managers-fail-and-how-to-prevent-it/?sh=6b43dd973385

[20]https://blackboardradio.com/blogs/how-to-be-a-master-presenter-5-lessons-from-steve-jobs/#:~:text=Practice%2C%20practice%2C%20and%20practice!,him%20deliver%20a%20flawless%20presentation.

[21] Schein, E. H. (1990). Organizational culture. American Psychologist, 45(2), 109-119. doi:10.1037/0003-066X.45.2.109

[22] Barney, J. B. (1986). Organizational culture: can it be a source of sustained competitive advantage?. Academy of management review, 11(3), 656-665.

[23] Barney, J. B. (1986). Organizational culture: can it be a source of sustained competitive advantage?. Academy of management review, 11(3), 656-665.

[24]https://knowyourmeme.com/memes/if-i-had-more-time-i-would-have-written-a-shorter-letter

[25] https://www.gallup.com/workplace/229424/employee-engagement.aspx

[26] file:///C:/Users/acraw/Downloads/state-of-the-global-workplace-2023-download.pdf

[27] Kahn, W. A. (1990). Psychological conditions of personal engagement and disengagement at work. Academy of Management Journal, 33(4), 692-724. doi:10.5465/256287

[28] Gallup. (2017). State of the American Workplace. Gallup.

[29] Helliwell, J. F., Huang, H., Grover, S., & Wang, S. (2019). Empirical Linkages Between Employee Well-Being and Business Success: A Review of the Evidence and Agenda for Future Research. Academy of Management Perspectives, 33(2), 183-205.

[30] Christian, M. S., Garza, A. S., & Slaughter, J. E. (2011). Work engagement: A quantitative review and test of its relations with task and contextual performance. Personnel Psychology, 64(1), 89-136.

[31] Parent, J. D., & Lovelace, K. J. (2015). The impact of employee engagement and a positive organizational culture on an individual's ability to adapt to organization change.

[32] Fidyah, D. N., & Setiawati, T. (2020). Influence of organizational culture and employee engagement on employee performance: job satisfaction as intervening variable. *Review of Integrative Business and Economics Research*, *9*(4), 64-81.

[33] Corporate Leadership Council. (2004). Driving Performance and Retention through Employee Engagement. Corporate Executive Board.

[34] https://www.amazon.com/Purpose-Driven-Life-What-Earth/

[35] https://positivepsychology.com/ikigai/

[36] https://www.linkedin.com/pulse/vic-clesceri/

[37] https://www.futuremarketinsights.com/reports/leadership-development-program-market

[38]https://hbr.org/2023/02/what-makes-leadership-development-programs-succeed#:~:text=One%20of%20the%20main%20ways,purpose%20at%20work%20and%20beyond.

[39]https://www.mckinsey.com/quarterly/the-five-fifty/five-fifty-employee-development-a-skills-based-approach

[40] Burns, D. D., & Beck, A. T. (1999). Feeling good: The new mood therapy.

[41] Dweck, C. S. (2006). Mindset: The New Psychology of Success. Random House.

[42]https://www.forbes.com/sites/robertamatuson/2023/07/27/is-executive-coaching-really-worth-the-money/?sh=725f60901664

Made in the USA
Columbia, SC
17 June 2024

36798432R00104